ABOUT ME

MY FULL NAME: _____

MY AGE: _____

MY HEIGHT: _____

MY FAVORITE COLOR: _____

I LOVE TO: _____

THINGS I LOVE ABOUT JESUS: _____
_____

I KNOW I SHOULD STUDY THE BIBLE BECAUSE: _____
_____

I AM EXCITED TO LEARN ABOUT: _____
_____

© 2022 by Carolyn Shuttlesworth

All rights reserved. No portion of this book may be reproduced, stored in a retrieval system, or transmitted in any form or by any means—electronic, mechanical, photocopy, recording, scanning, or other—except for brief quotations in critical reviews or articles, without the prior written permission of the publisher.

Published in Virginia Beach, Virginia by Miracle Word Publishing.

Miracle Word titles may be purchased in bulk for educational, business, fund-raising, or sales promotional use. For information, please e-mail info@miracleword.com

Scripture quotations marked (NLT) are taken from the Holy Bible, New Living Translation, copyright ©1996, 2004, 2015 by Tyndale House Foundation. Used by permission of Tyndale House Publishers, Carol Stream, Illinois 60188. All rights reserved

Scripture quotations are from the ESV® Bible (The Holy Bible, English Standard Version®), copyright © 2001 by Crossway, a publishing ministry of Good News Publishers. Used by permission. All rights reserved.

ISBN 978-1-7349962-4-1

Printed in the United States of America

STRONG SMART SET APART

Miracle Word Kids

TABLE OF CONTENTS

MONTH 1: THE BOOK OF PROVERBS	11
MONTH 2: GREAT FAITH	23
MONTH 3: PRAYER	37
MONTH 4: DECLARE IT	49
MONTH 5: ALL POWER	63
MONTH 6: FRUIT OF THE SPIRIT	75
MONTH 7: NEW TESTAMENT TRUTH	113
MONTH 8: FEAR NOT	125
MONTH 9: THANKSGIVING & PRAISE	139
MONTH 10: THE BOOK OF ACTS	173
MONTH 11: MY IDENTITY IN CHRIST	189
MONTH 12: THE BOOK OF LUKE	203

LETTER TO PARENTS

Hi, Parents!

Let me introduce myself. My name is Carolyn Shuttlesworth. I'm a homeschool mom of three children—Madelyn, Brooklyn, and Teddy III—who I teach on the go as my husband, Ted, and I travel and minister full time.

My heart's desire is for children to know and understand the Word of God at a young age. We launched Miracle Word Kids in November 2019. We've hosted free Bible studies, produced a large variety of topical videos from God's Word, had giveaways, online parties, released merch, and more! We've connected with kids from all over the world who write us and participate in all that we do.

The theme of Miracle Word Kids is based on a verse from the book of Luke. Chapter 2 shows us Jesus as a young boy spending time in the synagogues listening and speaking with the teachers. Even though he was full of wisdom at such a young age, it wasn't his time to step into ministry. He still had much to learn.

> **And the child grew and became strong, filled with wisdom. And the favor of God was upon him. – Luke 2:40**

Our children are a precious gift from God. They don't have to wait to be over 18 to be filled with the Holy Spirit or to gain revelation from God's Word. We need to immediately train our children to know what the Word of God teaches about faith, healing, prayer, their identity in Christ, being filled with the Holy Spirit, and more!

I pray this devotional creates a love for the Word inside of your children. As Christians, we should look different than those who don't have a Redeemer. Your kids will understand the critical role confession plays in their life. They will not fall prey to the lies of the enemy. They will be protected and walk in daily victory. Your kids will be Strong, Smart, and Set Apart!

Love, Carolyn

To my children—Madelyn, Brooklyn, and T3. You're the greatest possession the Lord has given to me. It's my life calling to teach you to walk in the abundance of the Lord. I love you with all of my heart.

INTRODUCTION

"THERE THE CHILD GREW UP HEALTHY AND STRONG. HE WAS FILLED WITH WISDOM, AND GOD'S FAVOR WAS ON HIM."
LUKE 2:40

Nothing is more important than knowing and obeying the Word of God. His Word gives us supernatural wisdom and direction. It should be the foundation for our entire life. The Bible is the instruction book for our lives! Nothing is higher than God's Word. It is the ultimate truth.

When you know and obey what the Word of God says, you become a dangerous force to the enemy. It's an unstoppable weapon that defeats him every single time. When you have a daily intake of the Word of God, the enemy will have no resources to take you out. Reading and memorizing the Word is food to your spirit man. It keeps you strong, smart, and set apart!

This 12-month Bible study will give you something different to read and study every day. You will know so much about what the Word of God says by this time next year! Anytime you see a megaphone, say the confession out loud. You will also see coloring pages and we want you to be creative!

We recommend reading from a New Living Translation Bible. Be sure to ask your parents when you need help! This is an interactive devotional so grab your pens. Are you ready? Let's go!

"Wisdom will multiply your days and add years to your life."

Proverbs 9:11

THE BOOK OF PROVERBS

The book of Proverbs is something that we should read daily for our entire lives. It's considered one of the Wisdom Books.

The purpose of this book is to teach wisdom to every single person. Having wisdom means that you will make good decisions and actions in your life because of what you know to be true. Wisdom will help keep you from making poor choices that you will regret. You are never too wise to gain the benefits found in the book of Proverbs. (See Proverbs 1:1-7.)

God has called us to live a certain way on the earth. Proverbs is a book of instructions on exactly how to do that. It gives us exceptional wisdom on living a happy, blessed, and peaceful life by honoring and respecting God. When we understand this principle, we will do the same towards our parents, teachers, pastors, and anyone put in authority over our lives.

A fun and unique thing about the book of Proverbs is that there are thirty-one chapters. Since there are usually thirty-one days in a month, it is easy to read one Proverb chapter per day. That's what we are going to do this month!

Every day you will read one proverb and then write your favorite verse that you read. Writing the Word of God will help you to remember what it says.

Day 1: Read Proverbs 1

Write Your Favorite Verse:

_____

_____

_____

Day 2: Read Proverbs 2

Write Your Favorite Verse:

_____

_____

_____

Day 3: Read Proverbs 3

Write Your Favorite Verse:

_____

_____

_____

Day 4: Read Proverbs 4

Write Your Favorite Verse:

_____

_____

_____

Day 5: Read Proverbs 5

Write Your Favorite Verse:

_____

_____

Day 6: Read Proverbs 6

Write Your Favorite Verse:

_____

_____

Day 7: Read Proverbs 7

Write Your Favorite Verse:

_____

_____

Day 8: Read Proverbs 8

Write Your Favorite Verse:

_____

_____

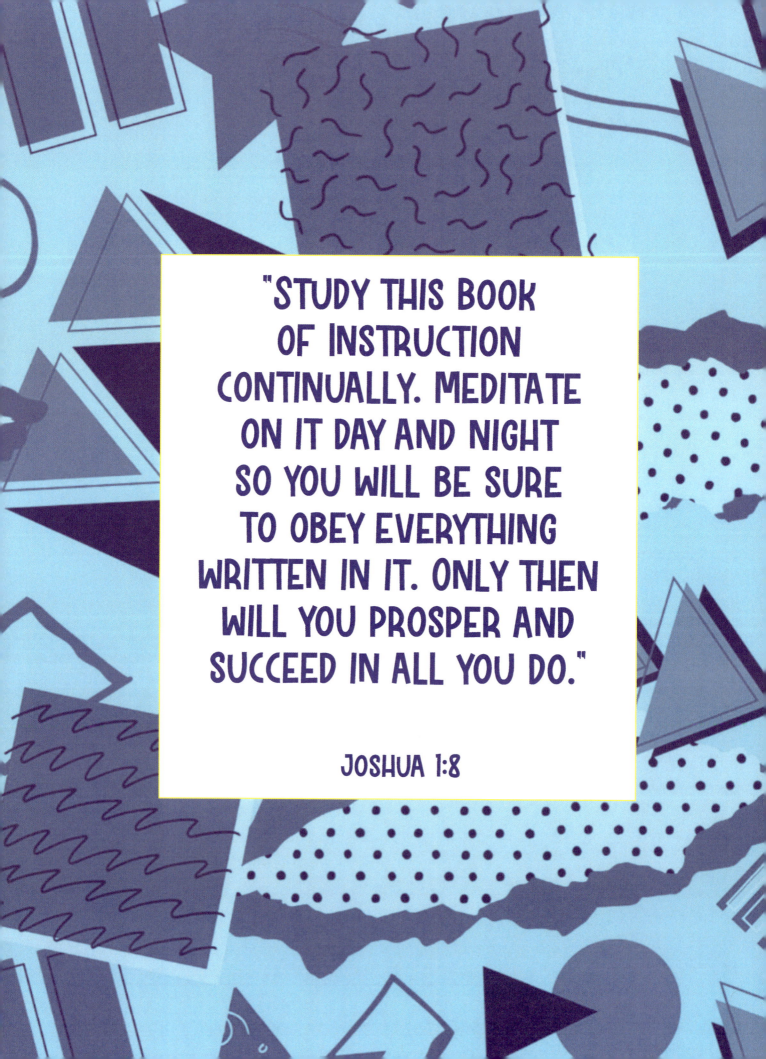

Day 9: Read Proverbs 9

Write Your Favorite Verse:

_____

_____

Day 10: Read Proverbs 10

Write Your Favorite Verse:

_____

_____

Day 11: Read Proverbs 11

Write Your Favorite Verse:

_____

_____

Day 12: Read Proverbs 12

Write Your Favorite Verse:

_____

_____

Day 13: Read Proverbs 13

Write Your Favorite Verse:

_____

_____

_____

Day 14: Read Proverbs 14

Write Your Favorite Verse:

_____

_____

_____

Day 15: Read Proverbs 15

Write Your Favorite Verse:

_____

_____

_____

Day 16: Read Proverbs 16

Write Your Favorite Verse:

_____

_____

_____

Day 17: Read Proverbs 17

Write Your Favorite Verse:

_____

_____

_____

Day 18: Read Proverbs 18

Write Your Favorite Verse:

_____

_____

_____

Day 19: Read Proverbs 19

Write Your Favorite Verse:

_____

_____

_____

Day 20: Read Proverbs 20

Write Your Favorite Verse:

_____

_____

_____

Day 21: Read Proverbs 21

Write Your Favorite Verse:

_____

_____

_____

Day 22: Read Proverbs 22

Write Your Favorite Verse:

_____

_____

_____

Day 23: Read Proverbs 23

Write Your Favorite Verse:

_____

_____

_____

Day 24: Read Proverbs 24

Write Your Favorite Verse:

_____

_____

_____

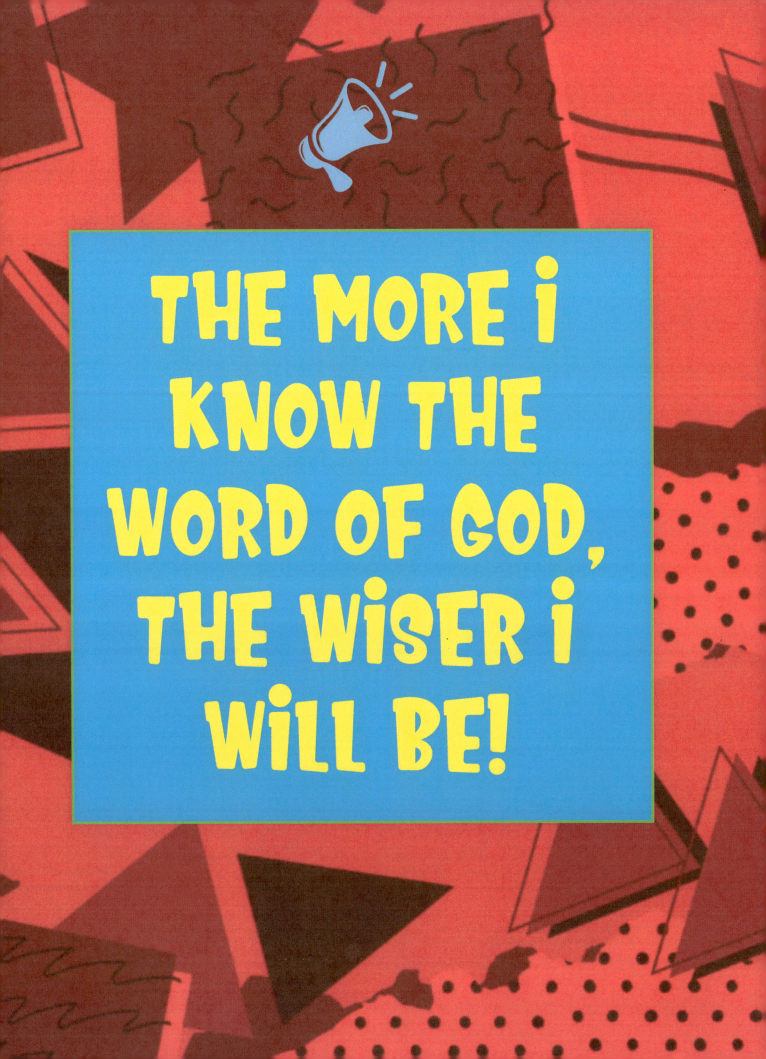

Day 25: Read Proverbs 25

Write Your Favorite Verse:

_____

_____

_____

Day 26: Read Proverbs 26

Write Your Favorite Verse:

_____

_____

_____

Day 27: Read Proverbs 27

Write Your Favorite Verse:

_____

_____

_____

Day 28: Read Proverbs 28

Write Your Favorite Verse:

_____

_____

_____

Day 29: Read Proverbs 29

Write Your Favorite Verse:

_____

_____

_____

Day 30: Read Proverbs 30

Write Your Favorite Verse:

_____

_____

_____

Day 31: Read Proverbs 31

Write Your Favorite Verse:

_____

_____

_____

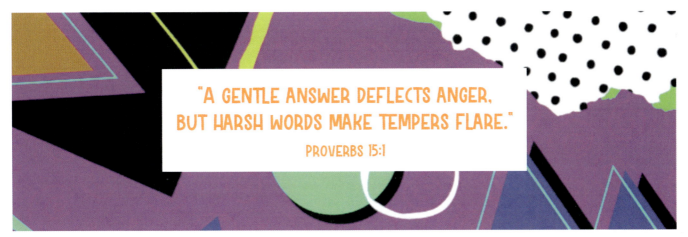

"A GENTLE ANSWER DEFLECTS ANGER, BUT HARSH WORDS MAKE TEMPERS FLARE."
PROVERBS 15:1

"And it is impossible to please God without faith. Anyone who wants to come to Him must believe that God exists and that He rewards those who sincerely seek Him."

Hebrews 11:6

GREAT FAITH

The Bible teaches us how to have great faith and believe to receive what God has promised us. That's what faith is! Faith is believing in God, and believing that everything he said in his Word is the truth!

God never lies to us. Everything he promised us in the Bible is true! When we have faith in God, we are showing him that we believe what he has told us. When we believe that everything in the Bible is true, it makes our faith so strong! Strong faith is very powerful. That's how we see miracles, signs, and wonders!

Jesus was perfect on the earth, and although we won't be as perfect as Jesus, Paul says in the Bible in 1 Corinthians 11:1, "And you should imitate me as I imitate Christ." We should act like him as best as we can. Jesus operated in great power on the earth. We are called to do the same, but it takes faith!

No matter how old you are, we're believing that your faith will go higher than it's ever been! God wants to use you mightily. You don't have to be a grown-up to have a powerful spirit. Let's learn what it takes to have great faith!

Day 1: Read Luke 8:40-55

Highlight Verses 46 and 48

How many years did the woman suffer?

_____

When she decided to get help from Jesus, did Jesus tell her he couldn't heal her, or did he heal her?

_____

What did her action of faith do?

_____

Day 2: Read Hebrews 11:1-12

Highlight Verse 1

Define faith:

_____

How do verses 1-11 start?

_____

By having faith, we can receive God's _____ . (Hint: starts with "p.")

Day 3: Read Matthew 6:28-34

Highlight Verses 31-33

What does God care about more? People, animals, or nature?

_____

If the animals and nature never have to worry if they will be provided for, do we?

_____

As a child of God, if we put the Kingdom of God first and live a righteous life, what will we get?

_____

Day 4: Read 1 Corinthians 16:5-18   Highlight Verses 13-14

Why do you think we are to be on guard?

_____

Who will come to try and steal from us?

_____

Why should we stand firm?

_____

Day 5: Read Matthew 8:23-27   Highlight Verses 26-27

How can you tell that Jesus had supernatural peace during the storm? (Hint: verse 25.)

_____

Is it possible to have different levels of faith? _____

Should we increase our levels of faith or remain where we are? _____

What did Jesus do in verse 26? _____

Did creation listen to Jesus? _____ Do we have the same authority? _____

Day 6: Read Romans 10:9-17   Highlight Verse 17

Who can be saved? (Hint: verse 13.) _____

In these verses, it tells us not everyone welcomes the gospel. It's important we do what? (Hint: verse 17.)

_____

How can we build our faith? (Hint: verse 17.)

_____

Day 7: Read Proverbs 3:1-12

Highlight Verses 5-6

How do you see faith working in the first six verses?

_____

What does it mean to trust?

_____

Does trusting take faith?

_____

Day 8: Read Luke 18:1-8

Highlight Verses 7-8

What did the widow want?

_____

Do we give up asking Jesus for help? _____

Did he die so we can have all he promised us? _____

When Jesus returns to the earth, will you be someone who is seen as having great faith? _____

Day 9: Read Mark 9:14-29

Highlight Verse 23

What was everyone in the crowd staring at?

_____

Why was Jesus aggravated? (Hint: verses 18 and 19.)

_____

If we believe (have faith), what are we able to do? (Hint: verse 23.)

_____

Day 10: Read Matthew 21:18-22

Highlight Verses 21-22

How can we compare this parable to our own life? _____

Trees are meant to produce. What does the tree represent?_____

What about the fruit?_____

Jesus operated in authority here by his words. What is the key thing we need to have to operate with such authority?

_____

Did he say we would end up having some things or everything we prayed for?_____

Day 11: Read Psalm 46:1-11

Highlight Verse 10

God dwells in the city, and it can't be destroyed. We represent the city. So if God lives in us, can we be destroyed?

_____

Do we need to be worried about bad things going on around us?

_____

Does having faith provide us peace? (Hint: verse 10.)_____

Day 12: 1 Thessalonians 5:1-24

Highlight Verses 23-24

What are we to be armed with? _____

What are we supposed to do to each other? _____

Can this help sharpen our faith by encouraging one another?

_____

What do we want God to call us? (Hint: verse 24.)

_____

Day 13: Read 2 Corinthians 5:1-10

Highlight Verse 7

What does it mean to be confident?

_____

How are we supposed to live? (Hint: verse 7.)

_____

Should we be constantly pleasing the Lord?

_____

Day 14: Read Romans 4:13-25

Highlight Verses 20-21

List some things that Jesus promised us:

_____

Abraham and Sarah couldn't have any children, but God said Abraham would be the father of many nations. Did it take faith to believe the Word of God?

_____

What does verse 21 say about Abraham? What was he? _____

Day 15: Read Romans 5:1-11

Highlight Verse 3

Because of our faith, where can we spend eternity?

_____

We have to have faith that Jesus is our Savior. Do you?

_____

Verse 11 says we can be a friend of God!

Salvation Prayer

If you don't know Jesus as your Savior or feel unsure if you're on your way to Heaven, repeat this prayer with your parents:

Jesus, I want to live in Heaven with you. I want to live in the promises that you have for me. I will let the Holy Spirit guide me and help me. I believe you died on the cross for me and rose on the 3rd day. I will not listen to the devil. He has no power because you have given it to me. You are Lord of my life!

Thank you, Jesus - I love you!

Day 16: Read James 1:1-18

Highlight Verses 5-8

If we need help from God, can we ask, or will he yell at us and tell us he is busy? _____

When we ask him, what are we to have? _____

If we don't fully believe, what does the Bible say we look like? Will we get our answer?

_____

Day 17: Read 1 Timothy 6:11-16

Highlight Verses 11-12

What six things should we pursue?

_____

_____

What are we not to do when we believe? (Hint: the word starts with a "w.")

_____

Day 18: Mark 10:46-52

Highlight Verses 51-52

Who is Bartimaeus?

_____

Why is he yelling for Jesus?

_____

Did Jesus ignore him or stop to help him?

_____

What does Jesus tell him in verse 52?

_____

Day 19: Read Psalm 119:30-48

Highlight Verse 30

FILL IN THE BLANK:

It is important we _____ His commands. I will put them into _____ with all of my _____ .

I will walk in _____ for I have _____ myself to your _____ .

Day 20: Read Mark 11:22-25

Highlight Verses 22-25

We are supposed to have the God kind of _____

What does it say we must really have? _____

Can we pray for certain things or anything? _____

Faith is an action word. So we must S _____ and B _____ .

Day 21: 1 Corinthians 13:1-13

Highlight Verse 13

After reading these thirteen verses, we find out that our faith works by:

_____

We can't have hate or unforgiveness. Our faith won't work. What are the three things that will last forever?

_____

Which is the greatest?

_____

Why? Because our faith can't work without:

_____

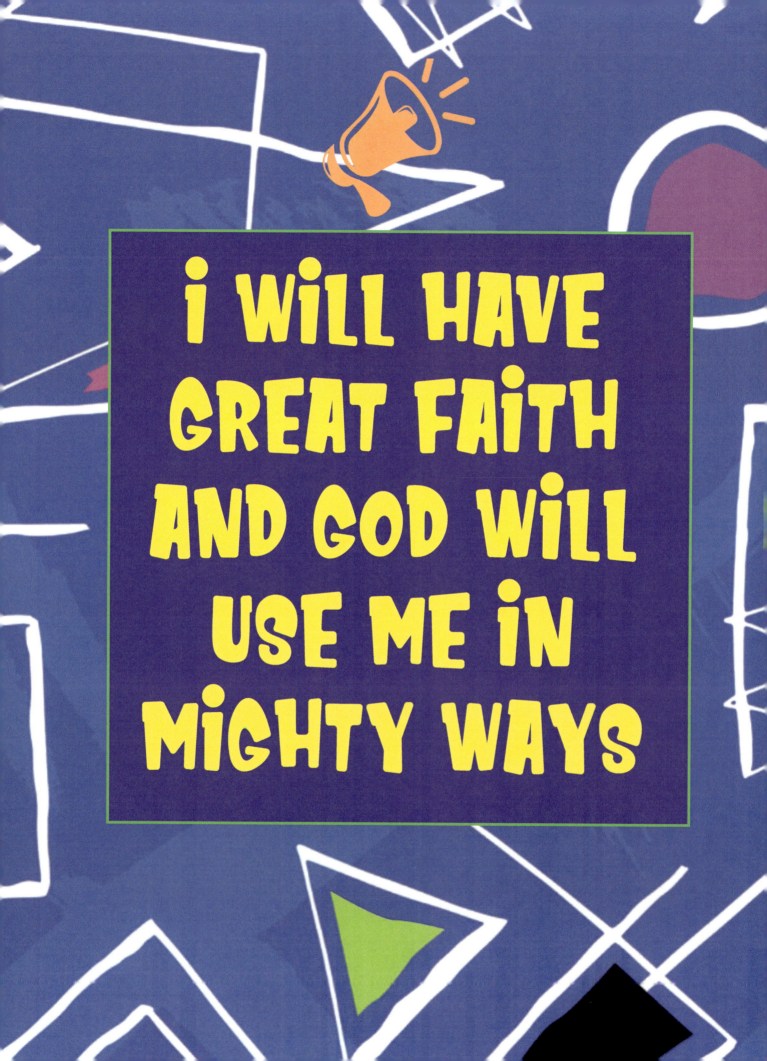

Day 22: Read John 7:37-39

Highlight Verse 38

Does it take faith to believe in Jesus?

_____

What will flow from us if we believe?

_____

Day 23: Read 2 Timothy 4:1-8

Highlight Verses 7-8

Is faith a fight? _____

Is it a fight we can win? _____

Who comes to fight us and steal from us? (Hint: John 10:10.)

_____

Day 24: Matthew 15:21-28

Highlight Verse 28

What was wrong with this lady's daughter?

_____

This woman wasn't a Jew; she was a Gentile. The disciples gave her a hard time because she wanted to get help from Jesus. His response didn't seem so nice, but she didn't get offended. Look at her response and discuss it with your parents. (Hint: verses 24-27.)

Her response caused Jesus to say she had GREAT FAITH! What happened to her daughter because of her great faith?

_____

"DEAR WOMAN," JESUS SAID TO HER, "YOUR FAITH IS GREAT. YOUR REQUEST IS GRANTED." AND HER DAUGHTER WAS INSTANTLY HEALED.
MATTHEW 15:28

Day 25: Read Luke 1:26-45　　　　　　　　　　　　　Highlight Verses 30, 35, 37, and 45

What was Mary told?

___

During this time, Elizabeth was also pregnant. Mary had found favor with the Lord, so when she went to visit Elizabeth, what did she say to Mary?

___

Day 26: Read Matthew 17:14-20　　　　　　　　　　　　　Highlight Verse 20

What was wrong with the boy? ___

What problem did the disciples have? (Hint: verse 16.) ___

What type of people does Jesus not want us to be like? (Hint: verse 17.) ___

Verse 20 shows us we can start with small faith to do large tasks. What do you think would happen if we kept growing our mustard seed size faith?

___

Day 27: Ephesians 2:1-10　　　　　　　　　　　　　Highlight Verses 8-10

What happened when Christ was raised from the dead?

___

How can we receive salvation? (Hint: verse 8.)

___

When we believe, will we have faith?

___

Day 28: Read Habakkuk 2:1-4

Highlight Verse 4

Do you think God gives us ideas to carry out?

_____

If he gives a vision, will he make it plain to us?

_____

Should we have faith to do what he's called us to do?

_____

Day 29: Read John 1:1-16

Highlight Verses 1-5

Does it take faith to believe verses 1 and 2?_____

Ever wonder who made God? There's a beginning to everything. God has always been the beginning (Genesis 1:1.) It takes faith to believe that! We have all been given a measure of faith, but it's our responsibility to grow it continually. That is our goal this month. There's no age limit to have great faith!

Day 30: Galatians 5:22-26

Highlight Verses 22-23

What are the nine kinds of fruit the Holy Spirit produces in our lives?

_____

_____

Should we pick and choose, or should we live by all nine?

_____

"Don't worry about anything; instead, pray about everything. Tell God what you need, and thank him for all he has done."

Philippians 4:6

PRAYER

This month we are going to take the time to pray. We are going to pray for our world, our family, our neighbors, and ourselves. Prayer is so important for Christians. It's talking directly to Jesus! You don't have to be in a special place to pray or pray in a funny voice to be heard. The Bible says to simply make your requests known to God.

One of the most important things you can learn about prayer, is praying according to God's Word. God's Word is his will, so when we make our prayers match what the Bible says, we know that God will do it for us!

Maybe you pray with a parent before you go to sleep at night, or before you eat your food. This month, we want to challenge you to pray more than you ever have before. Prayer is having a conversation with your Heavenly Father.

This study will teach you what to say when you talk to God. He loves you and wants you to talk to him! When your prayers match what the Bible says to be true, they become very powerful!

WEEK ONE

DAY 1: MY WORLD

THIS WEEK I WILL PRAY FOR THE NATION OF: _____

THESE ARE SOME THINGS I WILL PRAY ABOUT:

_____

_____

1 TIMOTHY 2:1-5

"I urge you, first of all, to pray for all people. Ask God to help them; intercede on their behalf, and give thanks for them. Pray this way for kings and all who are in authority so that we can live peaceful and quiet lives marked by godliness and dignity. This is good and pleases God our Savior, who wants everyone to be saved and to understand the truth. For, there is one God and one Mediator who can reconcile God and humanity—the man Christ Jesus."

DAY 2: MY COMMUNITY & NEIGHBORS

THIS WEEK I WILL PRAY FOR THE NATION OF: _____

THESE ARE SOME THINGS I WILL PRAY ABOUT:

_____

_____

1 JOHN 4:21

"And he has given us this command: Those who love God must also love their fellow believers."

WEEK ONE

DAY 3: MY FRIENDS

THIS WEEK I WILL PRAY FOR: _____

THESE ARE SOME THINGS I WILL PRAY ABOUT:

_____

_____

1 THESSALONIANS 5:11

"So encourage each other and build each other up, just as you are already doing."

DAY 4: MY FAMILY

THIS WEEK I WILL PRAY FOR: _____

THESE ARE SOME THINGS I WILL PRAY ABOUT:

_____

_____

JOSHUA 24:15

"But if you refuse to serve the Lord, then choose today whom you will serve. Would you prefer the gods your ancestors served beyond the Euphrates? Or will it be the gods of the Amorites in whose land you now live? But as for me and my family, we will serve the Lord."

WEEK ONE

DAY 5: MY COUNTRY

I LIVE IN THIS COUNTRY: _____

THESE ARE SOME THINGS I WILL PRAY ABOUT:

_____

_____

2 Chronicles 7:14

"Then if my people who are called by my name will humble themselves and pray and seek my face and turn from their wicked ways, I will hear from heaven and will forgive their sins and restore their land."

DAYS 6 & 7 : GIVE THANKS TO THE LORD

I AM THANKFUL TO GOD FOR THESE THINGS:

_____

_____

Psalm 86:12

"With all my heart I will praise you, O Lord my God.
I will give glory to your name forever."

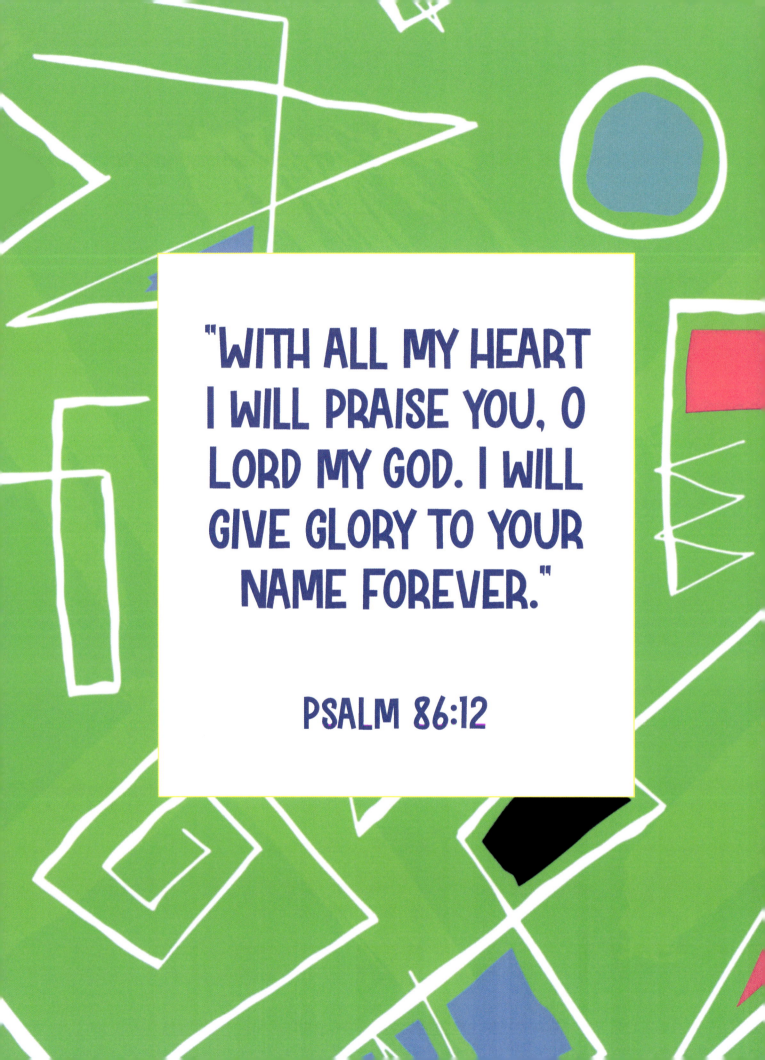

WEEK TWO

THESE ARE THE THINGS I WILL PRAY FOR:

DAY 8: WAYS I WILL PRAY FOR MY BROTHERS & SISTERS:

_____

_____

_____

_____

DAY 9: WAYS I WILL PRAY FOR MY MOM & DAD:

_____

_____

DAY 10: WAYS I WILL PRAY FOR MY PUBLIC SERVANTS. (POLICE, NURSES, TEACHERS, ETC.)

_____

_____

_____

_____

DAY 11: WAYS I WILL PRAY FOR MY CHURCH:

_____

_____

_____

DAY 12: WAYS I WILL PRAY FOR MYSELF:

_____

_____

_____

DAY 13 & 14: WAYS GOD HAS ANSWERED MY PRAYERS:

_____

_____

_____

_____

WEEK THREE

WRITE YOUR PRAYER LIST FOR EACH AREA.

DAY 15: MY SAFETY

_____

_____

READ PSALM 91

DAY 16: HEALTH

_____

_____

PSALMS 103:2-3
"Let all that I am praise the Lord; may I never forget the good things he does for me. He forgives all my sins and heals all my diseases."

DAY 17: MY FUTURE

_____

_____

JOHN 16:13
"When the Spirit of truth comes, he will guide you into all truth. He will not speak on his own but will tell you what he has heard. He will tell you about the future."

WEEK THREE

DAY 18: MY WANTS

_____

_____

PSALM 37:4
"Take delight in the Lord, and he will give you your heart's desires."

DAY 19: MY MIND

_____

_____

2 TIMOTHY 1:7
"For God has not given us a spirit of fear and timidity, but of power, love, and self-discipline."

DAY 20: SOULS
List 3 people that need to know Jesus and pray for them today!

_____

_____

JOHN 3:16
"For this is how God loved the world: he gave his one and only Son, so that everyone who believes in him will not perish but have eternal life."

Day 21 & 22:
TESTIMONIES

Write some of the ways God has answered your prayers so far this month:

WEEK FOUR: MY THANKFUL LIST

Each day this week, write at least three things that you're thanking God for. Make sure you tell God how thankful you are in your prayer time!

DAY 23: I AM THANKFUL FOR:

_____

_____

_____

DAY 24: I AM THANKFUL FOR:

_____

_____

_____

DAY 25: I AM THANKFUL FOR:

_____

_____

_____

DAY 26: I AM THANKFUL FOR:

_____

_____

_____

DAY 27: I AM THANKFUL FOR:

_____

_____

_____

DAY 28: I AM THANKFUL FOR:

_____

_____

_____

DAY 29: I AM THANKFUL FOR:

_____

_____

_____

DAY 30: I AM THANKFUL FOR:

_____

_____

_____

"The tongue can bring death or life; those who love to talk will reap the consequences."

Proverbs 18:21

DECLARE IT

This month we are going to learn about the power of our words. Each day, we are going to declare the Word of God together. We have given you declarations to say out loud, and a verse for you to read and write.

Declaring the Word of God is essential to our lives as Christians. Romans 10:17 says, "So faith comes from hearing, that is, hearing the Good News about Christ."

As we confess the things Jesus has said about us, our spirits grow. When the devil tries to lie to us, we will be so strong that he won't be able to trick us. We encourage you to write down each verse every day. That will help you to memorize Scripture.

Knowing the Word of God will make you strong, smart, and set apart!

Day 1:

SAY THIS: My words direct my life.

READ & WRITE: Proverbs 18:21

_____

_____

_____

Day 2:

SAY THIS: God is on my side. I can't be beaten.

READ & WRITE: Exodus 14:14

_____

_____

_____

Day 3:

SAY THIS: God will use me today to release his power and to love people around me.

READ & WRITE: John 14:12

_____

_____

_____

Day 4:

SAY THIS: I think right thoughts. I speak words of life and I make good decisions even when it is tough.

READ & WRITE: Psalm 19:14

_____

_____

Day 5:

SAY THIS: I am a leader. I have great ideas and God makes me powerful.

READ & WRITE: 1 Timothy 4:12

_____

_____

_____

Day 6:

SAY THIS: When I speak truth my faith grows, and I become who God made me to be.

READ & WRITE: Psalm 119:73-74

_____

_____

_____

Day 7:

SAY THIS: Because I love Jesus, angels are working for me.

READ & WRITE: Hebrews 1:14

_____

_____

_____

Day 8:

SAY THIS: Bad things turn away from me because of Jesus' protection.

READ & WRITE: Proverbs 18:10

_____

_____

_____

Day 9:

SAY THIS: I tell tiredness, sadness, and fear to leave in Jesus' name.

READ & WRITE: 2 Timothy 1:7

_____

_____

_____

Day 10:

SAY THIS: My health gets better everyday.

READ & WRITE: Romans 8:11

_____

_____

_____

Day 11:

SAY THIS: God loves to provide for me.

READ & WRITE: Matthew 6:31-33

_____

_____

_____

_____

Day 12:

SAY THIS: My prayers are powerful.

READ & WRITE: James 5:16

_____

_____

_____

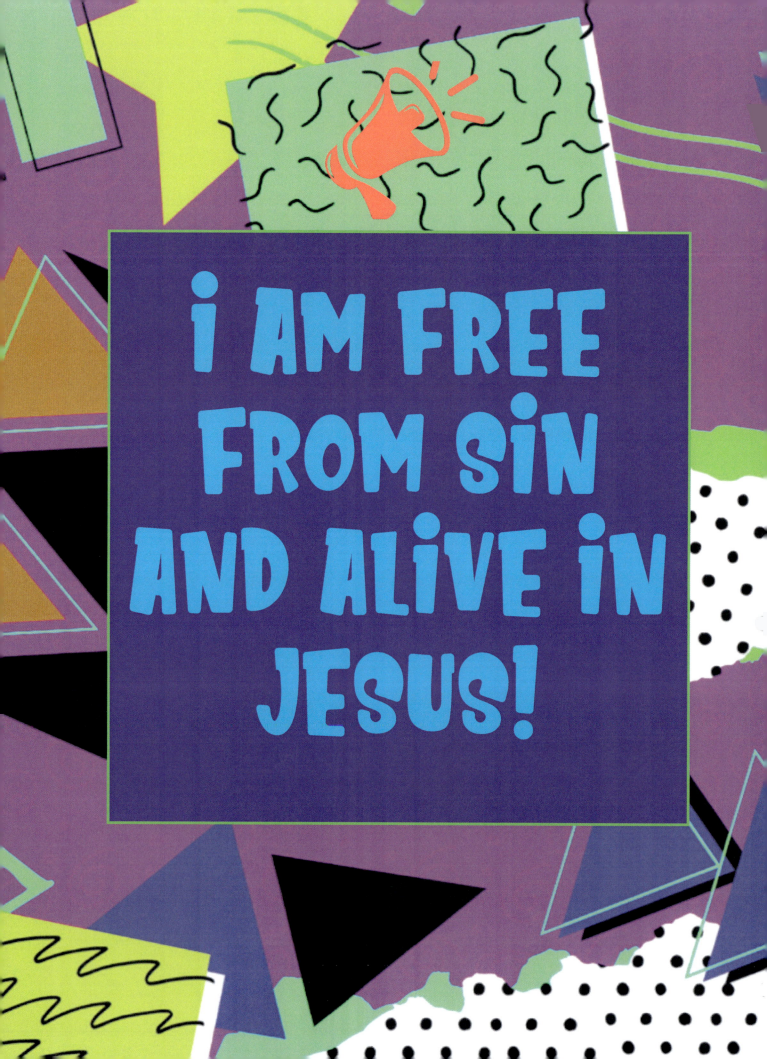

Day 13:

SAY THIS: I recognize and laugh at the devil's lies.

READ & WRITE: James 4:7

_____

_____

_____

Day 14:

SAY THIS: I am free from sin and alive in Him.

READ & WRITE: Romans 6:18

_____

_____

_____

Day 15:

SAY THIS: This day is a blessed day. I can't wait to see how God's goodness shows up.

READ & WRITE: Psalm 118:24

_____

_____

_____

Day 16:

SAY THIS: Because of Jesus, I am 100% loved and super blessed.

READ & WRITE: Romans 8:31-32

_____

_____

Day 17:

SAY THIS: I stand for what is right.

READ & WRITE: 1 Corinthians 16:13

_____

_____

Day 18:

SAY THIS: I am patient and self-controlled.

READ & WRITE: Galatians 5:22-23

_____

_____

_____

_____

Day 19:

SAY THIS: Even if I don't know the "right thing" to say, I will tell the truth.

READ & WRITE: Proverbs 12:22

___

Day 20:

SAY THIS: God loves the way I look and what he thinks matters most.

READ & WRITE: Ephesians 2:10

___

Day 21:

SAY THIS: Jesus is my healer.

READ & WRITE: Acts 10:38

Day 22:

SAY THIS: Because of my obedience, the Lord will take care of me.

READ & WRITE: Deuteronomy 28:1

_____

_____

_____

Day 23:

SAY THIS: I never have to worry. Jesus said he would take worry away.

READ & WRITE: 1 Peter 5:7

_____

_____

_____

Day 24:

SAY THIS: I will always be thankful no matter how I feel. I don't go by feelings. I will brag on his goodness.

READ & WRITE: Psalm 9:1

_____

_____

_____

Day 25:

SAY THIS: I am a person of peace and bring peace to those around me.

READ & WRITE: Isaiah 26:3

_____

_____

Day 26:

SAY THIS: Jesus has made me strong and courageous. I will not fail!

READ & WRITE: Joshua 1:9

_____

_____

Day 27:

SAY THIS: Jesus died just for me. He did it so I can live a wonderful life on earth and in Heaven.

READ & WRITE: John 10:10

_____

_____

_____

Day 28:

SAY THIS: Trouble leaves my heart because I believe in Jesus.

READ & WRITE: John 14:1

_____

_____

Day 29:

SAY THIS: God hears me when I talk to him.

READ & WRITE: Psalm 18:6

_____

_____

Day 30:

SAY THIS: I will obey my parents even when it doesn't feel easy.

READ & WRITE: Ephesians 6:1-3

_____

_____

_____

"And they sang in a mighty chorus: "Worthy is the Lamb who was slaughtered— to receive power and riches and wisdom and strength and honor and glory and blessing."

Revelation 5:12

ALL POWER

Jesus loves each one of us so much that he died on the cross so we could be saved and forgiven of all our sins. The death, burial, and resurrection of Jesus are very important to understand and celebrate all year long; not only on Easter.

In Revelation 5:12, the Bible tells us that because Jesus died on the cross for us and rose again, we receive seven redemptive benefits.

Jesus died so you could be powerful, so you could be wealthy, so you could be wise, so you could be mighty, so you could have honor, so you could have glory, and so you could have blessing!

This month we are going to read the Easter story in each Gospel. Take this month to understand why Jesus came to the earth and died for us. Take these next four weeks to study what Jesus did for us. Each day, describe why you're thankful.

He has done so much for us. Now we can live in freedom! You will learn of the power and presence of the Holy Spirit. He will give you guidance, power, and boldness to carry out all that God has for you in this life.

I AM POWERFUL
I AM WEALTHY
I AM WISE
I AM MIGHTY
I HAVE HONOR
I HAVE GLORY
I HAVE BLESSING

REVELATION 5:12

Week One
Read: Matthew 26-28

Day 1: Matthew 26:1-30

Day 2: Matthew 26:31-46

Day 3: Matthew 26:47-75

Day 4: Matthew 27:1-26

Day 5: Matthew 27:27-44

Day 6: Matthew 27:45-66

Day 7: Matthew 28

Week One Review

Now that you have read the Easter story from the Gospel of Matthew, what are some things you want to thank Jesus for today?

Thank You Jesus For:

_____
_____
_____
_____
_____
_____
_____
_____
_____
_____
_____
_____

Week Two
Read: Mark 15-16

Day 1: Mark 15:1-15

Day 2: Mark 15:16-24

Day 3: Mark 15:25-32

Day 4: Mark 15:33-47

Day 5: Mark 16:1-8

Day 6: Mark 16:9-14

Day 7: Mark 16:15-20

Week Two Review

Now that you have read the Easter story from the Gospel of Mark, what are some things you want to thank Jesus for today?

Thank You Jesus For:

___

___

___

___

___

___

___

___

___

___

Week Three
Read: Luke 22-24

Day 1: Luke 22:1-38

Day 2: Luke 22:39-53

Day 3: Luke 22:54-71

Day 4: Luke 23:1-25

Day 5: Luke 23:26-56

Day 6: Luke 24:1-35

Day 7: Luke 24:36-53

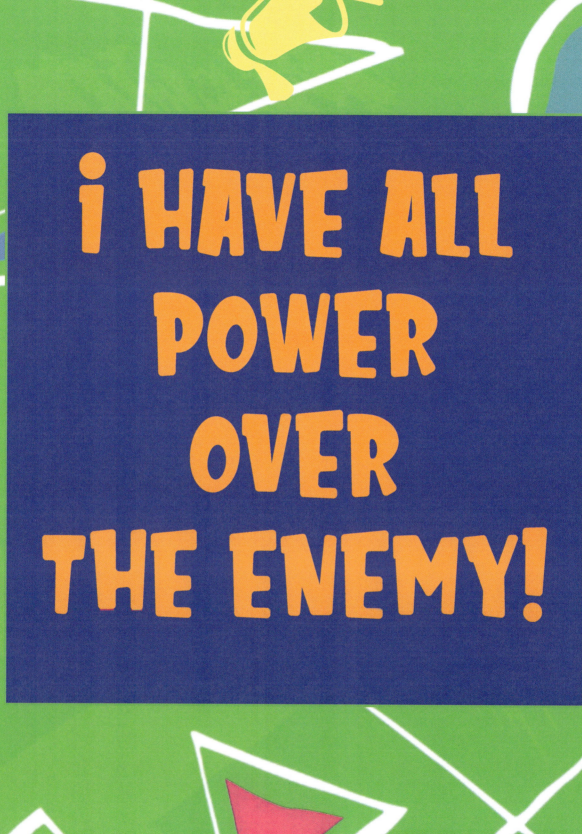

Week Three Review

Now that you have read the Easter story from the Gospel of Luke, what are some things you want to thank Jesus for today?

Thank You Jesus For:

_____
_____
_____
_____
_____
_____
_____
_____
_____
_____

Week Four
Read: John 17-20

Day 1: John 17

Day 2: John 18:1-27

Day 3: John 18:28-40

Day 4: John 19:1-16

Day 5: John 19:17-42

Day 6: John 20:1-18

Day 7: John 20:19-30

Week Four Review

Now that you have read the Easter story from the Gospel of John, what are some things you want to thank Jesus for today?

Thank You Jesus For:

_____
_____
_____
_____
_____
_____
_____
_____
_____
_____

"But the Holy Spirit produces this kind of fruit in our lives: love, joy, peace, patience, kindness, goodness, faithfulness, gentleness, and self-control. There is no law against these things!"

Galatians 5:22-23

THE FRUIT OF THE SPIRIT

In this month, we are going to go through the fruit of the Spirit each week. We'll get a closer look at their importance and see why it's imperative we have them in our lives.

The Bible tells us in Galatians 5 that the Holy Spirit produces nine different fruit.

They are LOVE, JOY, PEACE, PATIENCE, KINDNESS, GOODNESS, FAITHFULNESS, GENTLENESS, AND SELF-CONTROL.

We not only want to be a good witness of our Savior Jesus Christ, but we want to see good things happen in our own life.

Have you ever seen rotten fruit? It's mushy, bruised, smelly, and it becomes inedible. Same for us! If we don't show love, joy, peace, patience, kindness, goodness, faithfulness, gentleness, and self-control, we become like rotten fruit. It will be easy to believe the lies of the enemy.

So each week this month, we are going to take time to learn about each fruit.

9 FRUIT OF THE SPIRIT

LOVE — JOY — PEACE

PATIENCE — KINDNESS — GOODNESS

FAITHFULNESS — GENTLENESS — SELF-CONTROL

WEEK ONE | PART ONE

WHAT DOES THE BIBLE SAY ABOUT LOVE?

Love is a powerful thing. It's not just a fruit of the Spirit; it is a command by God. Read Matthew 22:37-40. We are to love even if the other person doesn't love us back. We have to make sure we focus on what the Lord wants us to do. When we live in obedience, we live in the blessing (1 Samuel 15:22).

Write: John 15:12-13

_____

_____

Love in us produces selflessness. We weren't even around yet, but Jesus still died on the cross for us. He gave up his life for the future you. That is pretty selfless to die for someone you don't even know! He died so you can live free from sin, disease, fear, anxiety, anger, and so much more!

What are some other things Jesus died for?

_____

_____

When we learn to love no matter what, that kind of love opens the door to all the fruit of the Spirit. When we have love, the other fruit of the Spirit will come easy to us.

Let's Think About it!

The next time you start to feel upset, stop and think about your reaction. Did you follow 1 Corinthians 13? Were you rude? Did you get upset because things didn't go your way? Did you stay mad and not forgive?

How can you show love this week to the people in your life, whether it's your parents, brother, sister, friend, or someone you don't even know very well?

_____

_____

_____

Find Another Verse in the Bible About Love and Write it Below:

_____

_____

Prayer This Week:

Jesus, help me to love as you love us. Help me to show love every day, even when I don't feel like it. I will allow the Holy Spirit to be my leader. I truly love you, Jesus, and I want to be a good representation of your love to everyone I meet.

WEEK ONE | PART TWO

HOW DO WE GET JOY?

Joy comes from being with Jesus! Joy is not just about a smile on our face. A lot of times, we may have a smile on our face but not be happy. Joy is a smile on the inside of us, and no matter what is going on around us, we still choose joy.

It's a choice we have to make despite how we feel. Do you think Jesus felt joyful about dying on the cross? Read Mark 14:35-36. Jesus did all that for you so he could experience joy watching you live on this earth receiving all that he has for you, operating in his power, and bringing you to Heaven.

Write: PSALM 16:11

_____

_____

The more time we spend with Jesus, the more joy we will have. Jesus is the source of our joy! That's why it's important we take time to read his Word, memorize what he is saying, be filled with the Holy Spirit, and pray.

What is something you can start doing today that you haven't done before? Set a goal!

_____

_____

Write: John 15:10-12

_____

_____

_____

_____

Just like when we took the first half of this week to learn about love, we can tie in joy with the other fruit of the Spirit. Our joy will be so full when we love as Jesus loves. Being with him is how we have joy. It's a strength to us and helps us in doing all that he commands.

If we love others (not their bad actions that go against God's Word), but love people, his joy will be in us. Be so full today that it can't help but get on someone else around you!

What can you do today to share your joy with others?

_____

_____

_____

_____

Let's Think About it!

Do you ever let your feelings take control of your attitude? Do you wear your feelings on your face?

_____

What happens if you stop spending time with Jesus?

_____

Find Another Verse in the Bible About Joy and Write it Below:

_____

_____

_____

Prayer This Week:

Jesus help me to choose joy. The Bible says I am filled with the same Spirit as Christ, and I want that characteristic to grow in my life. Use me to bring joy to others around me.

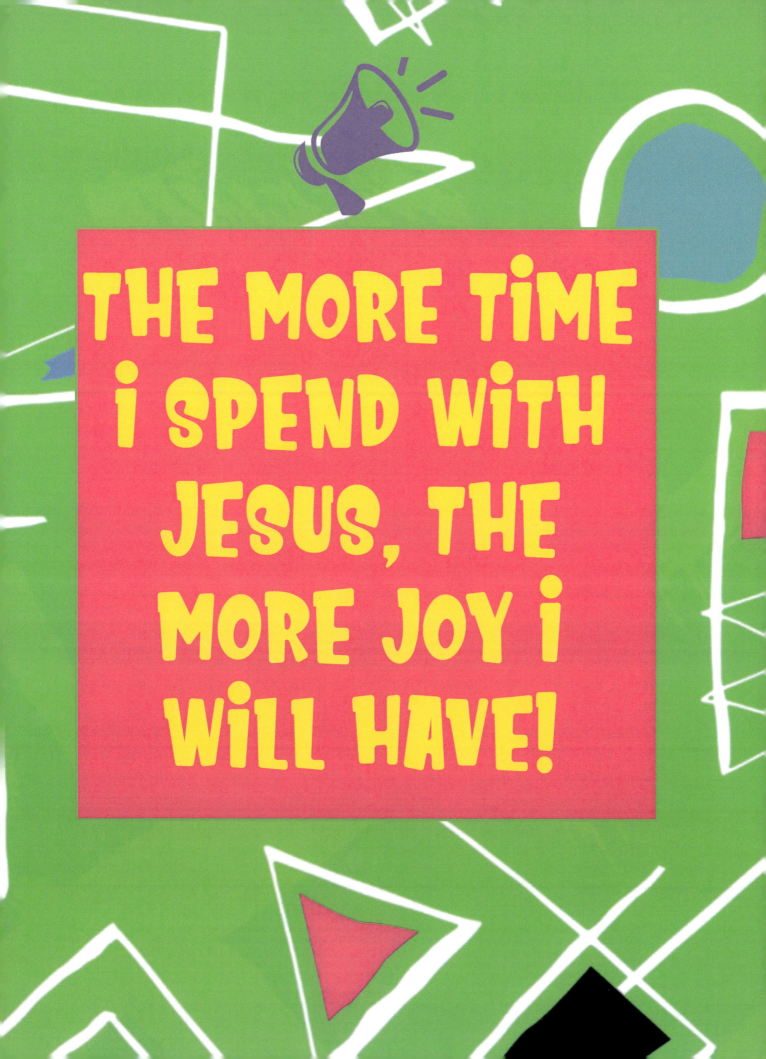

WEEK TWO | PART ONE

What does the Bible say about Peace?

In Isaiah, we read that if we keep our mind (our thoughts) on him and put total trust in what he says, we will be in perfect peace! As a Christian, we can trust that God is in control. We never have to worry, fear bad things, or feel like he isn't around for us. It's true even when things around us may feel out of control. Living in the peace of God means we are able to remain calm.

Write: Isaiah 26:3

_____

_____

_____

Here is a story from Mark 4. It shows Jesus is our ultimate restorer of peace. Everywhere he went when he lived on earth, he restored peace. Turn to Mark 4:35-41 and read the story. Jesus and his disciples were on a boat crossing the Sea of Galilee. Jesus went to go to sleep. During his sleep, a fierce storm started. Jesus stayed asleep until they woke him up.

Think about it. These are professional fishermen. They are used to boats and storms, but this one filled them with such fear they felt like they were unable to do anything about it except wake Jesus for help. Jesus was certain that nothing bad would happen to them. He woke up and brought peace to the storm and peace to his disciples.

Why do you think this scary storm didn't wake Jesus?

_____

Write: John 14:27

_____

_____

_____

Understanding this verse from the book of John is extremely important. We have to see what it's telling us. Peace is a gift from Jesus. When you give a gift to a friend, does someone else have the right to take it away from them? NO! This gift has a name tag with your name on it.

We need to do what the Bible says. You must learn to live in peace with your surroundings and have peace on the inside. You have to be fully convinced that no matter what you may see or experience around you, everything is going to be okay.

No situation slips past Jesus. If you feel worried, or lack inner peace, it's because you don't believe God is able to take care of you or that he even wants to.

Remember this:

"And we know that God causes everything to work together for the good of those who love God and are called according to his purpose for them." Romans 8:28.

Be certain today that everything is going to be okay! You are a kingdom kid, and he wants the best for his children!

Let's Think About it!

Is there something you feel concerned about? Does Jesus care about every detail of our life?

_____

What do you have to do to live in perfect peace?

_____

When others around you feel upset, what can you say to help calm them?

_____

Find Another Verse in the Bible About Peace and Write it Below:

_____

_____

Prayer This Week:

Dear Lord, I want to live in peace. I want my family to feel your peace. Thank you for taking all my concerns away. I will trust in your Word and know that you love me so much and want your best for me.

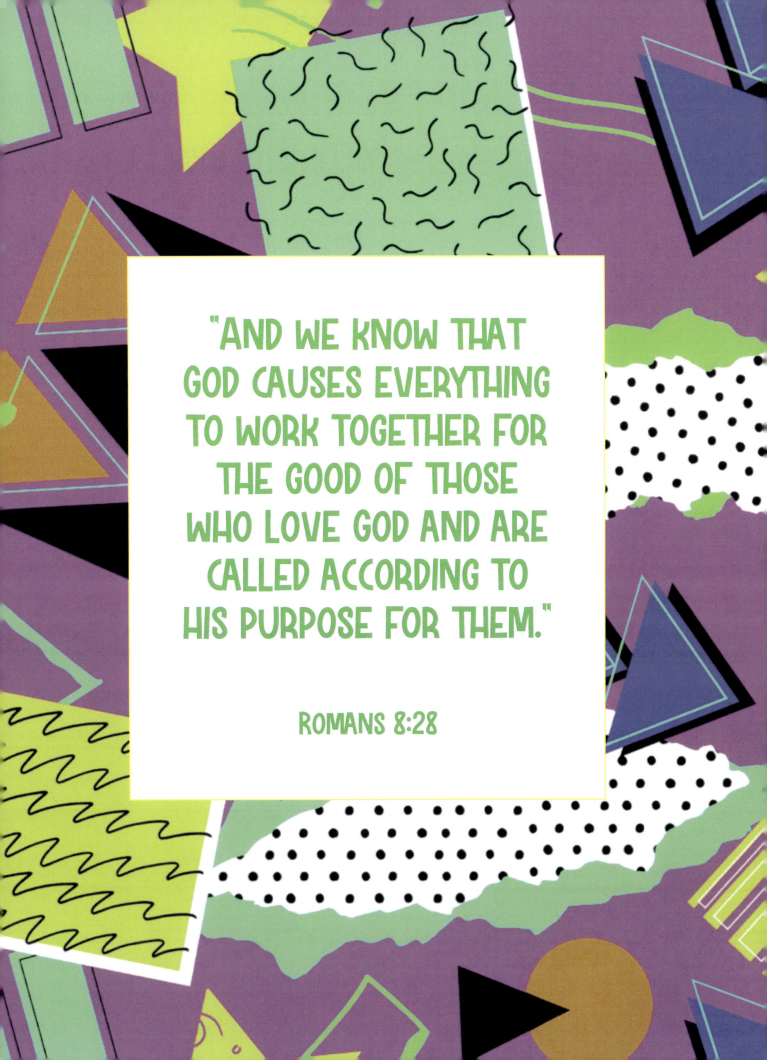

WEEK TWO | PART TWO

What does the Bible say about Patience?

Let's read Psalm 37:7.

"Be still in the presence of the Lord, and wait patiently for him to act."

If God said he would do it, he will not forget. This week you will learn a story where waiting would have seemed impossible, but because they were obedient and waited patiently for God to act, they were protected.

Patience is being able to wait for something without being annoyed or restless. If you want to play with the toy your friend has, will you be patient? If you have been waiting a long time to play your new video game, but your brother is still using it, how will you react?

Write: 2 Peter 3:15

_____

_____

_____

We all know the story of Noah and the Flood, but did you know that Noah waited over 100 years until the rains started? Say what?!? Over 100 years of waiting from when the Lord told him what to build. That took supernatural patience.

Did he say, "I've been building this ark for years and haven't seen any rain clouds. I'm done. Everyone is watching me and thinks I'm crazy! I'm old and tired, and I don't want to do this anymore!" No! He continued to do as the Lord instructed him.

Why do you think Noah had such amazing patience? He truly believed that God always keeps his promises and that God's timing is perfect. Only when there's a lack of trust can we become impatient, but that's not the case with our Heavenly Father.

Just look what Numbers 23:19 says: "God is not a man, so he does not lie. He is not human, so he does not change his mind. Has he ever spoken and failed to act? Has he ever promised and not carried it through?"

Complete confidence in the Word of God gives us patience. Here are some good things that will happen to those who are willing to wait:

Write: Philippians 4:19
(Our needs are met!)

_____

_____

Write: James 1:5
(We get wisdom!)

_____

_____

Write: John 14:2-3
(Jesus will come back to the earth!)

_____

_____

Let's Think About it!

What does it look like to be patient in your grade? Could it be a good attitude when someone cuts you in line?

_____

What if you're tired of telling your friend about Jesus? Do you give up on them?

_____

Does Jesus keep his promises?

_____

Find Another Verse in the Bible About Patience and Write it Below:

_____

_____

Prayer This Week:

Dear Jesus, I will trust your promises because you never lie. When I ask for things from you, I will be patient to receive. When you tell me to do something, I will be patient to finish it like Noah. God has given me the Holy Spirit to remind me I can do all things through Christ.

WEEK THREE | PART ONE

What does the Bible say about Kindness?

Ephesians 4:32 instructs us, "Instead, be kind to each other, tenderhearted, forgiving one another, just as God through Christ has forgiven you."

It doesn't say be kind to someone else who was kind to you first. The Bible simply tells us to be kind. What does it mean to be kind? Why do you think kindness is a fruit of the Spirit? Jesus is kind, and when his Spirit lives in us, he teaches us to be kind to others.

Write: Proverbs 3:3

_____

_____

Let's look at the Good Samaritan. This story is found in Luke 10:30-37. A man was traveling alongside the road to Jerusalem, when two robbers attacked. He was beaten and robbed. He was so badly hurt he lay on the side of the road, unable to get up.

While the man lay helpless on the road, a priest and a Levite at two separate times came along the same path. They looked at him and kept going. But then the third man, a Samaritan, came over to the man and saw how he looked and felt. He picked him up and placed him on his donkey. He brought him into the town, cleaned him up, and bandaged his wounds.

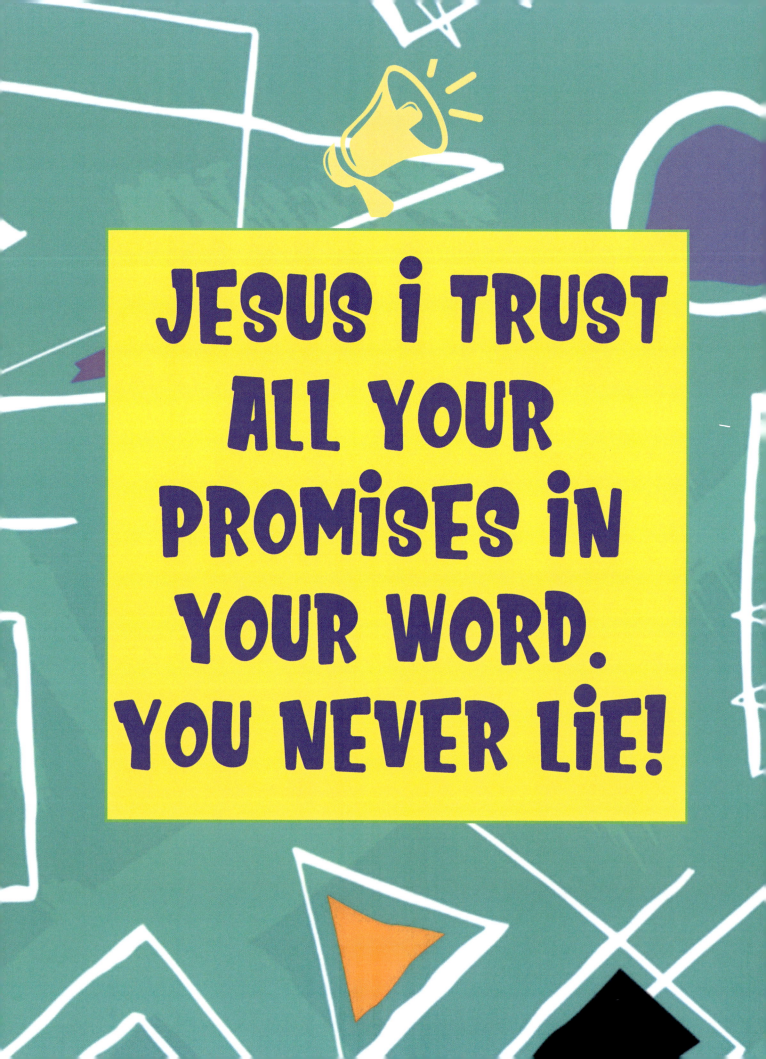

This Samaritan man showed kindness to a complete stranger. Would you do that? Would you take extra time out of your busy day to help someone in need? Would you take your own money to help someone you don't know?

Jesus instructs us in verse 37 that we are to go and act the same way the Samaritan acted. Sometimes we want only to be nice to people if we get something from them. Jesus was kind to all. He showed love and kindness even to his enemies.

Kindness isn't always the "popular" thing to do, but it's the right thing to do.

Write: 1 Thessalonians 5:15

_____

_____

_____

Let's Think About it!

Is it easy to be kind? Are you ever tempted to be unkind? Who does Jesus say we are to be unkind to? When we are kind to others, is it a good way to share God's love with them?

_____

What are some ways that Jesus shows kindness to you?

_____

This week choose some acts of kindness around your house, school, and neighborhood. For example, bring up your neighbor's trash cans from the street or help around with some house chores you wouldn't normally do.

Find Another Verse in the Bible About Kindness and Write it Below:

_____

_____

Prayer This Week:

Thank you, Jesus, for showing me so much kindness through your Word. You died for our sins so we can live forever with you. You heal our body. You keep me and my family protected. Help me to be more like you. You are so good to me. Thank you, I love you.

WEEK THREE | PART TWO

What does the Bible say about Goodness?

We can see in James 1:17, "Whatever is good and perfect is a gift coming down to us from God our Father, who created all the lights in the heavens. He never changes or casts a shifting shadow."

Just the very beginning of that verse shows you that every good and perfect gift comes to us from our Heavenly Father. We should be keeping our thoughts on his goodness.

Write: Psalm 23:6

_____

_____

Throughout the Bible, we are shown Jesus' goodness to the believer. While he lived on the earth, he showed goodness to everyone he came in contact with. We can see one example in Matthew 4:23-25.

It said because of his goodness, they knew he would heal them. Some had demons, some suffered from a lot of pain, couldn't stop shaking, and others couldn't move. But Jesus healed them all! All of these great miracles caused large crowds to follow him.

In a world full of pain and suffering, he brought good to it. His GOODNESS goes far beyond if we even deserve it. He does it because of his great love. Can you see how all the fruit of the Spirit are tied together? You must have and show all nine. We can't pick and choose.

Write: Philippians 4:8

_____

_____

_____

In order for us to produce goodness, we have to make sure our insides are pure. If you have goodness in your life, others around you can see it and want what you have. But if you spend all your time not thinking about the right things, you won't produce the right fruit. You can't sugarcoat sin.

When we have bad fruit, eventually, the rotten inside begins to show on the outside. Keep yourself fixed on what pleases your Savior. Then what's on the inside of you must come out, and others will want to know the God you serve!

Let's Think About it!

Will the things I watch and listen to produce goodness in my life? How can I show others God's goodness in my life?

_____

What are some ways that Jesus has showed me and my family his goodness?

_____

_____

_____

Find Another Verse in the Bible About Kindness and Write it Below:

_____

_____

_____

Prayer This Week:

Thank you, Jesus, for always showing me your goodness in my life. Help me to be strong in the things of God. I want to be pleasing to you.

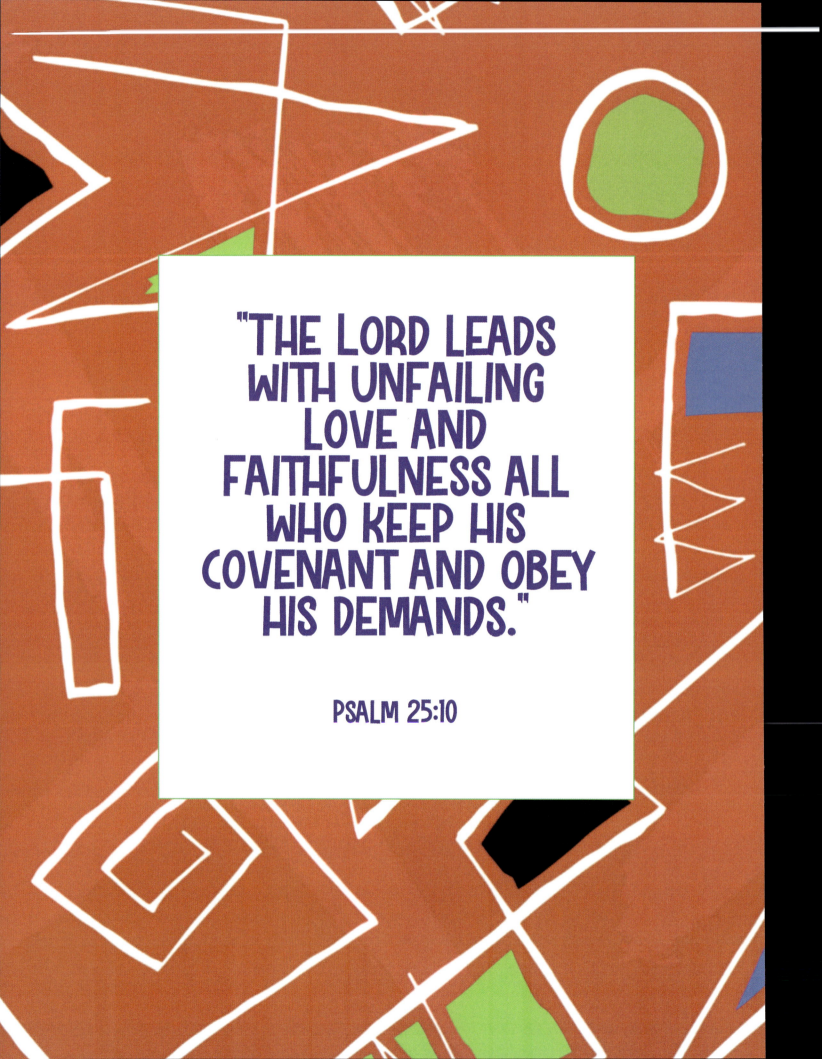

"The Lord leads with unfailing love and faithfulness all who keep his covenant and obey his demands."

PSALM 25:10

WEEK THREE | PART THREE

What does the Bible say about Faithfulness?

Deuteronomy 7:9 says, "Understand, therefore, that the Lord your God is indeed God. He is the faithful God who keeps his covenant for a thousand generations and lavishes his unfailing love on those who love him and obey his commands."

That should make you leap for joy! Our Heavenly Father is faithful, which means you can always count on him! Since faithfulness is a fruit of the Spirit, the Holy Spirit produces it in you when you choose to follow Jesus. You can also be faithful to him!

Faith is when you put your trust in Jesus. Faithfulness is the action of continually obeying the Word of God. You are full of faith!

Write: Psalm 25:10

_____

_____

After Jesus died on the cross, rose from the dead, and ascended to Heaven, people had the opportunity to become Christians. Not everyone was happy about that, and this made people very mean towards Christians.

Do you think when someone makes fun of what you believe, you should change your belief? Or stay faithful to our Lord?

Open your Bible to Acts 11:19-26. You see, in verse 19, Christians had to leave quickly from Jerusalem because the Jews were unhappy with the teachings of Jesus. The Bible uses the word persecution. That means hostility and ill-treatment, especially because of race, political, or religious beliefs. These new Christians had to make a choice to remain FAITHFUL to Jesus even during difficult times.

Is this how you would be?

_____

Write: PSALM 108:4

_____

_____

_____

When you go through the book of Joshua, you can see God's people, the Israelites, faced many, many challenges. It took them a long time to get to the Promised Land. It may have even crossed their mind that God forgot about his promise to them.

Joshua 21:45 says, "Not a single one of all the good promises the Lord had given to the family of Israel was left unfulfilled; everything he had spoken came true."

He remained faithful to them, and he will remain faithful to you.

Let's Think About it!

Is there something you are praying for that you haven't seen an answer to? Don't give up! As long as you line up your words with the Word of God, it has to be answered! You do your part and remain faithful, and Jesus will do his part and stay faithful. Jesus believes in you and has great plans for you!

How are you applying faith to your daily living?

_____

_____

Find Another Verse in the Bible About Faithfulness and Write it Below:

_____

_____

_____

Prayer This Week:

Dear Jesus, thank you for being so faithful to me. I will not doubt your Word. I will continue to believe and receive all that you have for me.

WEEK FOUR | PART ONE

What does the Bible say about Gentleness?

It says in Colossians 3:12, "Since God chose you to be the holy people he loves, you must clothe yourselves with tenderhearted mercy, kindness, humility, gentleness, and patience."

Gentleness is something we must "wear" every day. The Word of God wants all of our reactions in life to be gentle. Have you ever heard someone tell you, "Don't say it like that, your tone wasn't very nice. You sounded angry."

Although you may not be feeling super angry at that moment, your voice made the other person receive a rough answer.

Write: Proverbs 15:1

_____

_____

Do you realize how powerful your words are? God created this world by words, and look how long it has lasted and will continue to last. Those are some pretty powerful words!

We have to think before we speak. The Bible says in James 1:19, "Understand this, my dear brothers and sisters: You must all be quick to listen, slow to speak, and slow to get angry. Our words can be harsh or our words can be gentle."

Let's look at the story in 1 Kings 12:12-17. Rehoboam was a harsh and cruel king. The Israelites, also known as Jews, had become used to living under the authority of harsh kings or rulers. In fact, when Zechariah lived, the Jewish people had just been released from living in slavery in Babylon and had been allowed to go back to Jerusalem.

Zechariah encouraged the people by telling them that they could look forward to the coming of another king. He told them the coming king would bring salvation and righteousness. He also said the new king would be gentle.

Who was Zechariah talking about?

When Jesus did come, he told the people he was gentle and humble and that he would carry their burdens and give them a light "yoke" (Read Matthew 11:28-30.) He reminded them that he would not be a harsh and cruel ruler but a kind and gentle leader.

Jesus came to save the Jewish people from their sins, and he came to do that for you, too! Our Heavenly Father is not harsh to us. He is gentle in all of his ways towards us.

Write: Ephesians 4:2

_____

_____

_____

_____

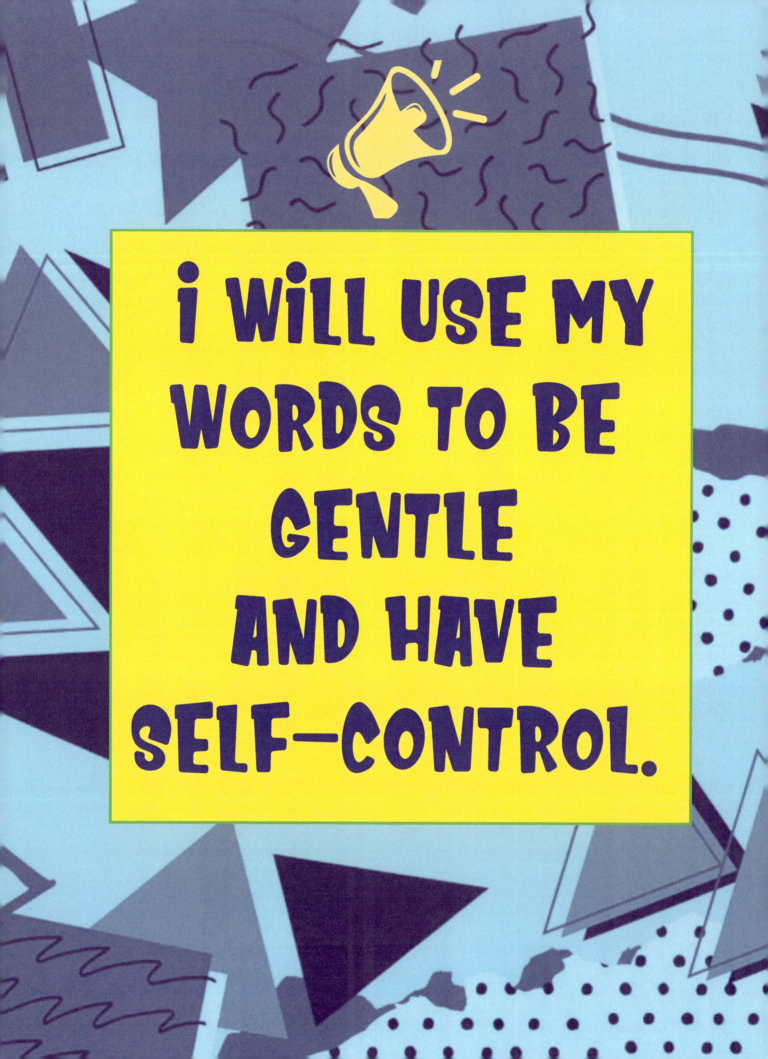

Let's Think About it!

Do your words show that you care about the other person? Do they come out as frustration or anger? Were you quick to listen, so you knew what the other person was saying and slow to respond?

_____

What is something you can work on this week that will show people you are gentle (like in Ephesians 4:2) even when they make a mistake?

_____

_____

Find Another Verse in the Bible About Gentleness and Write it Below:

_____

_____

_____

Prayer This Week:

Jesus, help me to use my words to be gentle. Give me self-control to be quick to listen but slow to answer. I want my words to represent you. I want people to know you're my Jesus by the words that come out of my mouth.

WEEK FOUR | PART TWO

What does the Bible say about Self-Control?

The Bible is pretty serious about this fruit. This is one of the most important fruit of the Spirit. If we can truly live by this fruit, all the other fruit of the Spirit will come much easier.

It says in Proverbs 5:23, "He will die for lack of self-control; he will be lost because of his great foolishness."

We have to be willing to use God's Spirit to help control our thoughts and our actions. We are to be imitators of Christ (1 Corinthians 11:1). Jesus not only had the self-control to keep him from doing wrong things, but his self-control also kept him always doing the right thing!

Write: Titus 2:12

_____

_____

You have to learn to control your "want to's." Through self-control, you keep yourself from doing something bad that you shouldn't do, and you make yourself do good things that you should do.

You might think, "Well, Jesus must have lived a life very different from me. He didn't have to live with my sister or brother!" We might think that no one ever bothered him, or nothing ever went wrong for him. This is not true at all. He had a family too. He had to deal with the different personalities of his family and friends, and strangers around him.

Jesus showed us the ultimate act of love and self-control when he went to the cross. Let's look at Mark 14:35-36. He prayed that, if it were possible, that the awful hour awaiting him might pass by. "Abba, Father," he cried out, "everything is possible for you. Please take this cup of suffering away from me. Yet I want your will to be done, not mine."

No one just wants to go through a horrible beating then finish it off with nails through your body and hanging on a cross. But by his incredible self-control, Jesus chose to obey God's will rather than doing what he wanted to do. That's the purest form of self-control.

Think about all the power that Jesus had. He did many miracles— he healed the sick, created food to feed thousands, and cast out demons. He even raised people from the dead! Could Jesus have stopped the soldiers and the people from nailing him to that cross? Yes! Of course! Jesus had all the power of his Father at his fingertips.

Write: Proverbs 25:28

_____

_____

_____

_____

Jesus always had the self-control to keep himself from sin and to obey God. The reason he had this amazing self-control was that he was full of the Holy Spirit, and he spent as much time as he could with his Father.

The more time we spend with God, the more good fruit God will grow in our lives – and Jesus had the most spiritual fruit of anyone!

Let's Think About it!

Can we be like Jesus? Can we choose to be more patient with a friend? Speak kindly to our brother or sister? Love a grumpy neighbor?

_____

What are some ways you can show self-control this week? What can you work on to show self-control?

_____

_____

Find Another Verse in the Bible About Self-Control and Write it Below:

_____

_____

_____

Prayer This Week:

Dear Jesus, give me self-control in all of my decisions. I want to make you proud and obey your Word. Help me to be a good listener to my parents and my teachers. I will be faithful to your Word and I will choose joy and peace around me. I love you so much Jesus. Thank you for dying on the cross for me even though I wasn't around then. I want to love like you love.

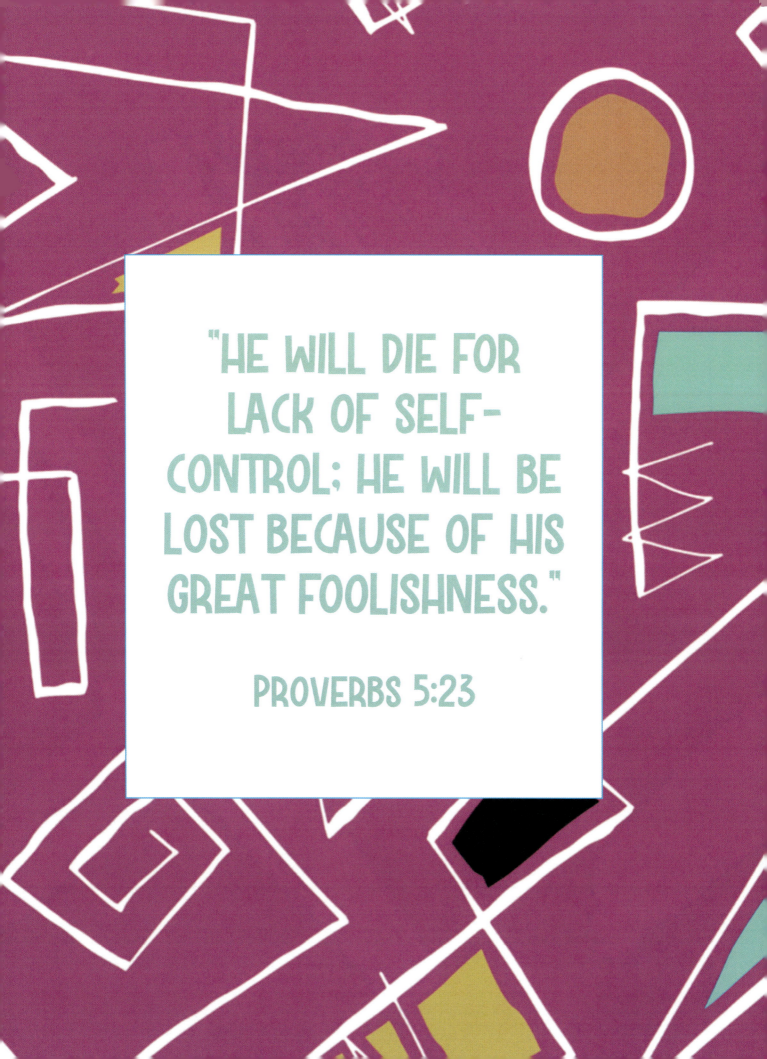

Let's Review!

The fruit of God's Spirit grows and grows in us as we remain with Jesus. How can we do that? As we talk to him, listen to him, and read his word. Love, joy, peace, patience, kindness, goodness, faithfulness, gentleness, and self-control grow in us and show in us because of our relationship with Jesus.

Write the correct word on the line from the word bank:

For hints: Use the NLT to look up any verses but try to answer before looking it up!

WORD BANK

LOVE   JOY   PEACE   TREASURE   PEACE

PATIENTLY   GOODNESS   KINDNESS   FAITHFULNESS

GALATIANS   CONVICT SIN

INSTRUCTION IN RIGHTEOUSNESS AND SOUND JUDGMENT

1. What is the role of the Holy Spirit? _____ (John 16:8)

2. The fruit of spirit is love, joy, peace, patience, kindness, goodness, faithfulness, gentleness, and _____. (Galatians 5:22)

3. Your laws are my _____; they are my heart's delight. (Psalm 119:111)

4. Do all that you can to live in _____ with everyone. (Romans 12:18)

5. Great is his _____; his mercies begin afresh each morning. (Lamentations 3:23)

6. But you, Timothy, are a man of God; so run from all these evil things. Pursue righteousness and a godly life, along with faith, love, perseverance, and_____. (1 Timothy 6:11)

7. The Lord is merciful and compassionate, slow to get angry and filled with unfailing_____. (Psalm 145:8)

8. The Lord is righteous and everything he does; is filled with _____.(Psalm 145:17)

9. Don't be dejected and sad, for the_____ of the Lord is your strength! (Nehemiah 8:10)

10. Be still in the presence of the Lord, and wait _____ for Him to act. Don't worry about evil people who prosper or fret about their wicked schemes. (Psalm 37:7)

11. Yet I am confident I will see the Lord's _____ while I am here in the land of the living. (Psalm 27:13)

12. The book of the Bible where Paul mentions the fruit of the Spirit _____

"Now all glory to God, who is able, through his mighty power at work within us, to accomplish infinitely more than we might ask or think."

Ephesians 3:20

NEW TESTAMENT TRUTH

When we read the Word of God, it's important to not just think of it as a regular book or even a good story. When we read God's Word, we should always ask ourselves, "How can I apply this to my life?"

God always has truth to tell us when we read the Bible. One of the cool things about the Word of God is that you can learn something different every time you read it. You can read the same verse many different times, but God can show you something different about himself each time!

You can never read too much of the Word. There's no such thing as knowing everything the Bible teaches. God has something new for you every time you read or listen.

This month, we are going to be reading a lot of the New Testament. It's important to say what the Word of God says. Each day, you will have reading to do, and truth to say out loud. This is learning how to apply the Word of God to your life. You will be strong, smart, and set apart!

Day 1:

READ: Galatians 1-2

SAY THIS:

Jesus Christ lives inside of me!
He loves me very much and gave his life for me.
(Galatians 2:20)

Day 2:

READ: Galatians 3-4

SAY THIS:

Because Jesus died on the cross for me, I can have the blessings of Abraham. I am an heir!
(Galatians 3:19,29)

Day 3:

READ: Galatians 5-6

SAY THIS:

I have the fruit of the Spirit in me today and that includes love, joy, peace, patience, kindness, gentleness, goodness, faithfulness, and self-control.
(Galatians 5:22)

Day 4:

READ: Ephesians 1-2

SAY THIS:

Jesus is in charge, and higher than anything or anyone.
(Ephesians 1:22)

Day 5:

READ: Ephesians 3-4

SAY THIS:

God is able to do more than I can even think or imagine!
(Ephesians 3:20)

Day 6:

READ: Ephesians 5-6

SAY THIS:

I am obedient to my parents and listen to their instruction.
(Ephesians 6:1-2)

Day 7:

READ: Philippians 1-2

SAY THIS:

I am not selfish, or only think of myself. I think of others too, and how I can love as Jesus loves them.
(Philippians 2:3)

Day 8:

READ: Philippians 3-4

SAY THIS:

I do not worry about anything. When I pray, God will give me peace and take all worry and fearful thoughts away.
(Philippians 4:6)

Day 9:

READ: Colossians 1-2

SAY THIS:

Wisdom and knowledge about who God is will be like treasure to me. Knowing him is more important than anything!
(Colossians 2:2-3)

Day 10:

READ: Colossians 3-4

SAY THIS:

I think about things that please God and make him happy. I don't think about things that make me afraid, sad, or things that don't matter.
(Colossians 3:2)

Day 11:

READ: 1 Thessalonians 1-2

SAY THIS:

The Holy Spirit gives me so much joy!
(1 Thessalonians 1:6)

Day 12:

READ: 1 Thessalonians 3-4

SAY THIS:

Jesus is coming soon, and I will tell other people how much God loves them and wants them to be saved!
(1 Thessalonians 4:16)

Day 13:

READ: 1 Thessalonians 5 and 2 Thessalonians 1

SAY THIS:

I will rejoice and praise the Lord always! He is always good!
(1 Thessalonians 5:16)

Day 14:

READ: 2 Thessalonians 2-3

SAY THIS:

I will never get tired of doing what is good and pleasing to the Lord.
(2 Thessalonians 3:13)

Day 15:

READ: 1 Timothy 1-2

SAY THIS:

God wants every person to be saved.
(1 Timothy 2:4)

Day 16:

READ: 1 Timothy 3-4

SAY THIS:

Even though I am young, I can be a good example to others in how I talk and act. Other people will know Jesus loves them because of me!
(1 Timothy 4:12)

Day 17:

READ: 1 Timothy 5-6

SAY THIS:

God gives me things that I enjoy because he loves me.
(1 Timothy 6:17)

Day 18:

READ: 2 Timothy 1-2

SAY THIS:

I will have self-control over my behavior. I will be kind to everyone.
(2 Timothy 2:24)

Day 19:

READ: 2 Timothy 3-4

SAY THIS:

The Bible is the Word of God. It is the most important instruction I can follow. When I obey what the Bible says, it will only bring me good.
(2 Timothy 3:16)

Day 20:

READ: Titus 1, 2, 3

SAY THIS:

I will not be someone who causes fights or arguments. I say and do things that please the Lord.
(Titus 3:10)

Day 21:

READ: Philemon

SAY THIS:

I think about and pray for other people, not just for myself.
(Philemon 1:4)

Day 22:

READ: Hebrews 1-2

SAY THIS:

If I feel tempted to do something wrong, Jesus will help me.
(Hebrews 2:18)

Day 23:

READ: Hebrews 3-4

SAY THIS:

The Bible is like a sharp sword- it is powerful! Reading and knowing God's Word makes me strong, smart, and set apart.
(Hebrews 4:12)

Day 24:

READ: Hebrews 5-6

SAY THIS:

I will keep learning the Word of God so that I am stronger and wiser everyday.
(Hebrews 5:13-14)

Day 25:

READ: Hebrews 7-8

SAY THIS:

Because of what Jesus did on the cross, I can live free from all sin and live in all his blessings.
(Hebrews 8:6)

Day 26:

READ: Hebrews 9-10

SAY THIS:

The blood of Jesus takes away all of my sins!
(Hebrews 10:10)

Day 27:

READ: Hebrews 11

SAY THIS:

Faith pleases God very much and my faith will increase everyday as I study and hear the Word of God.
(Hebrews 11:1)

Day 28:

READ: Hebrews 12

SAY THIS:

God's kingdom cannot be shaken. No one is stronger than God, and because he lives in me, I am strong too!
(Hebrews 12:28)

Day 29:

READ: Hebrews 13

SAY THIS:

The Lord always helps me. I never have to be afraid!
(Hebrews 13:6)

Day 30:

READ: James 1-2

SAY THIS:

God will give me wisdom so I can be smart and make right choices.
(James 1:5)

"The Lord is my shepherd; I have all that I need. He lets me rest in green meadows; He leads me beside peaceful streams. He renews my strength. He guides me along right paths, bringing honor to His name."

Psalms 23:1-3

FEAR NOT

This month, we are going to look up verses on what the Bible says about being afraid, anxious, or worried. Jesus died on the cross so we don't have to have those feelings. His Word promises us protection and peace.

Every day this month, you will have verses to read and discussion questions to answer. Take this time to really understand what the Bible says about fear. Before you read, pray and ask the Lord to give you wisdom and revelation of the scriptures you are reading. That will light up your spirit man with truth of his Word and you will remember it forever.

Joshua 1:8 says, "Study this Book of Instruction continually. Meditate on it day and night so you will be sure to obey everything written in it. Only then will you prosper and succeed in all you do."

The world may say that being afraid or worried is normal, but that's not true when you're a Christian! Jesus wants us to live in peace and joy all the time. He never wants you to be afraid and has given you everything you need in his Word so that you never have to be!

Day 1: Read John 14:23-31

Highlight Verses 26 and 27

Who are the ones that will be obedient?

_____

Who is Jesus sending that will be our helper and teacher?

_____

Jesus gave us a special gift that the world can't take away. What is that gift?

_____

Day 2: Isaiah 41:8-20

Highlight Verse 10

We are told not to be afraid. Why?

_____

We don't ever have to worry about being without. Jesus will always provide during any season.

Day 3: Read Joshua 1:5-16

Highlight Verses 8 and 9

What are we to study? _____

Why? _____

If we are fully obedient, only then what will happen?

_____

_____

Day 4: Read 2 Timothy 1:5-18

Highlight Verse 7

What gives us boldness? (Hint: It's a person.)

___

Does fear come from Jesus or the devil?

___

What three things did Jesus give us ?

___

Day 5: Read 1 Corinthians 16:5-18

Highlight Verses 13 and 14

Who is talking to us in chapter 16?

___

He gives us five instructions on how we should act. What are the five instructions?

___

___

Day 6: Read Psalm 34:1-22

Highlight Verses 4 and 5

How can we live a long and prosperous life?

___

___

Day 7: Read Deuteronomy 31:1-8

Highlight Verse 6

What does Moses let the people know? Who is taking his place to lead the Israelites?

_____

Moses gives the same instruction in verses 6 and 8? What was it?

_____

_____

Day 8: Psalm 112:1-10

Highlight Verses 7 and 8

What type of fear do they describe? Scary fear or speaking of honor?

_____

What should we delight in?

_____

Fear of God means having a specific sense of respect, awe, and submission.

Day 9: Read Hebrews 13:1-14

Highlight Verse 6

Will Jesus ever change? _____

We are considered ambassadors. An ambassador is an official representative for a foreign country. Where do we belong? (Hint verse 14.)

_____

_____

Day 10: Read Philippians 4:1-9

Highlight Verse 6 and 7

What should we always be full of?

_____

Instead of worrying what should we do?

_____

Day 11: Read Isaiah 12:1-6

Highlight Verse 2

What three things is the Lord God to us?

_____

What should we tell the world?

_____

Can we tell the world if we have fear?

_____

Day 12: Read Revelation 1:12-19

Highlight Verse 17

Can you describe what the Son of Man looked like?

_____

What is the first thing he tells us to do in verse 17?

_____

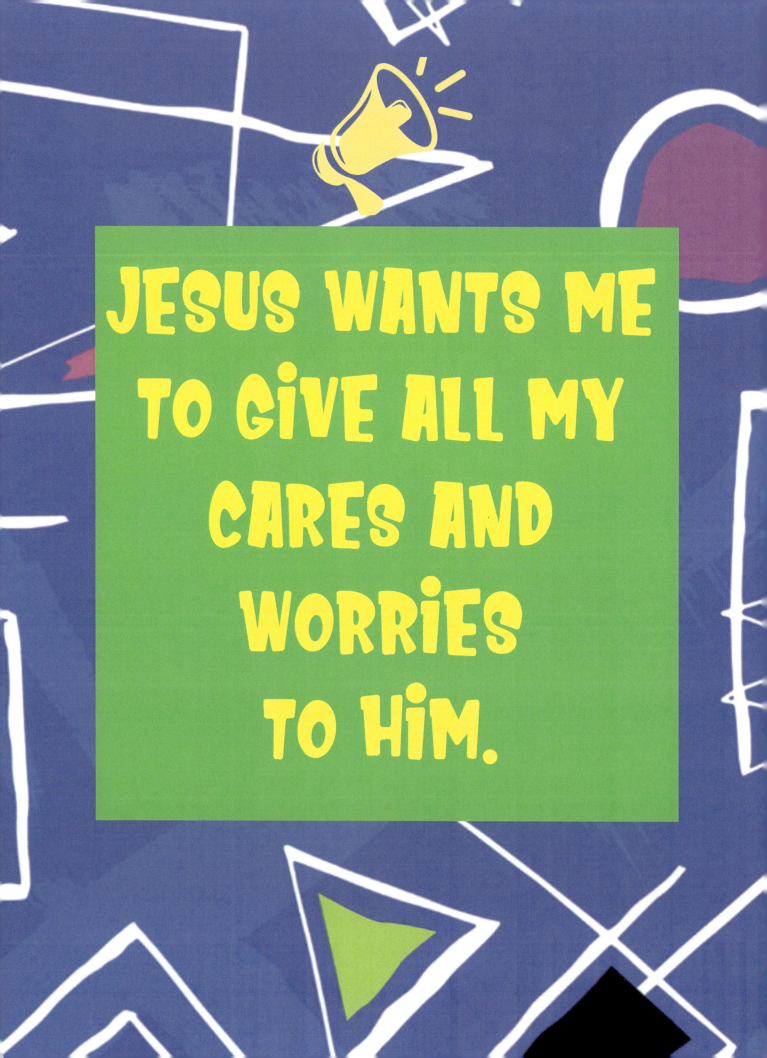

Day 13: Read 2 Chronicles 20:1-30

Highlight Verse 20

What is happening with King Jehoshaphat?

___

What was the outcome of the war?

___

Who won and how?

___

Day 14: Read Psalm 27:1-14

Highlight Verse 1

What kind of person is in chapter 27?

___

How are we to act?

___

Day 15: Read John 14:1-14

Highlight Verse 1

How can we get to Heaven?

___

Will we do the same works as Jesus did on earth?

___

Why?

___

Day 16: Read Isaiah 44:1-28

Highlight Verses 1-5

What does this say about idols?

Why is it so bad to have idols?

What does the Lord say about himself?

Day 17: Romans 8:1-16

Highlight Verses 15 and 16

If we are dominated by our sinful nature, what will we think of?

If we are controlled by the Holy Spirit, what will we think of?

If we let the Holy Spirit be our helper and guide should we be scared, fearful of things, or panic in situations?

Day 18: Read Psalm 91:1-16

Highlight Verse 1-16

Where should we live? Why?

Does this chapter say "sometimes" you'll be protected from everything sent to bother you?

What are your favorite parts in this chapter and why?

Day 19: Read Matthew 6:25-33

Highlight Verses 25 & 32, 33

What are these verses showing you?

_____

Do the animals worry about what they will have?

_____

Do we need to worry? Will God always provide for us? What do we need to seek and how should we live?

_____

Day 20: Read Luke 1:26-45

Highlight Verses 30, 35 & 37

What happened to Mary?

_____

Even though she was scared of the unknown for a moment, what did the angel reassure her with?

_____

Why is verse 37 so important to remember?

_____

Day 21: Read Matthew 7:9-11

Highlight Verse 11

Do we have to worry about our life?

_____

Did God promise to take care of us? _____

What is our part in order to have this good future? (Hint verse 11.)

_____

Day 22: Read Isaiah 35:1-10

Highlight Verse 4

Do we ever have to fear the devil?

Does the devil have more power than Jesus? Does the devil have more power than you?

Day 23: Genesis 15:1-21

Highlight Verse 1

What did Abram want but didn't have?

Did God promise this and why?

Day 24: Read Psalm 3:1-8

Highlight Verse 6-8

Does this chapter say we can sleep in peace?

Why don't we have to be afraid?

What will God do to our enemies?

Day 25: Psalm 27:1-14

Highlight Verses 1, 13 & 14

Why shouldn't we fear after reading this chapter? List some reasons.

_____

Should we use the Bible as our way to learn how to live? (Hint: verse 11.)

_____

Day 26: Read Mark 5:35-43

Highlight Verse 36

What happened to the little girl in the story?

_____

Did Jesus freak out? How did he respond?

_____

These verses show us not to have fear but to have what?

_____

Day 27: Read Daniel 10:1-12

Highlight Verse 12

In Daniel's vision what good news does the messenger have for him?

_____

_____

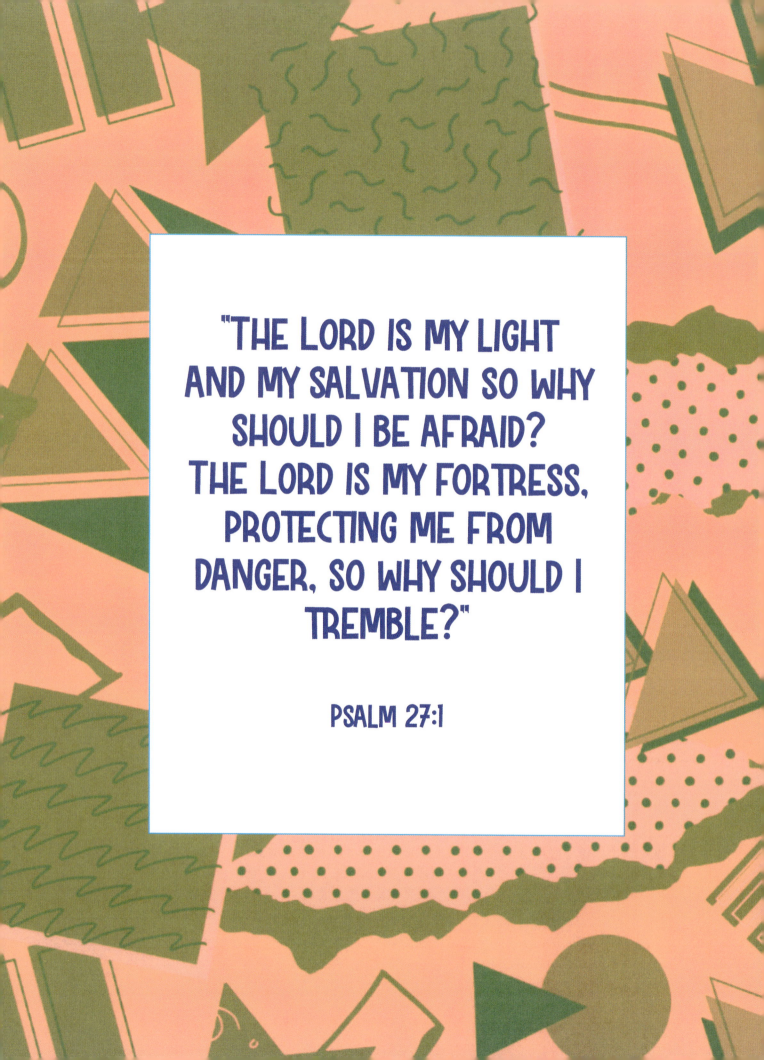

"The Lord is my light and my salvation so why should I be afraid? The Lord is my fortress, protecting me from danger, so why should I tremble?"

Psalm 27:1

Day 28: Read 1 Chronicles 28:1-21

Highlight Verse 20

Why did David want to build the temple?

_____

What did he want to put in it?

_____

Day 29: Read Acts 27:13-25

Highlight Verse 22

If things around us are not going well, how can we remember to act? (Hint: This is what Paul told the crew.)

_____

_____

Day 30: Read Psalm 23:1-6

Highlight Verses 1-6

What does this chapter show us?

_____

Is Jesus always with us?

_____

Will he always take care of us?

_____

"Always be joyful, never stop praying. Be thankful in all circumstances, for this is God's will for you who belong to Christ Jesus."

1 Thessalonians 5:16-18

THANKSGIVING & PRAISE

This month we are going to take each day to read what the Bible says about being thankful and praising our Lord and Savior. You'll learn that no matter what, he is always faithful.

Even if you're having a bad day. His love, goodness, peace, and faithfulness are always there for you.

Have you ever given a gift to a friend, but they never said anything about it? You may have felt hurt, annoyed, or angry. Just think how Jesus feels if he never hears from you! You have to remember to acknowledge him daily. Not just for what he's already done in your life, but for what he's about to do too!

This month you will have daily reading along with some questions to answer. Each day say out loud or write down something you are thankful for. By the end of the month you'll be able to go back and really see all of God's goodness in your life in just one month!

DAY 1

READ PSALM 95:1-7

> WHAT DOES BEING THANKFUL MEAN?

> WHAT DO THESE VERSES SAY ABOUT BEING THANKFUL TO GOD? WHOSE ARE YOU?

> HOW DID YOU ENJOY GOD'S CREATION TODAY?

> NAME ONE THING YOU ARE THANKFUL FOR TODAY AND ASK YOUR PARENT THE SAME QUESTION.

DAY 2

READ EPHESIANS 2:4-9

YOU READ YESTERDAY THAT GOD CREATED YOU, THE WORLD, AND EVERYTHING IN IT. WHAT OTHER GIFT DID GOD GIVE YOU?

WHY DID GOD GIVE YOU THIS GIFT? (VERSE 4)

WHAT DO THESE VERSES TEACH YOU ABOUT WHY YOU SHOULD BE THANKFUL TO GOD?

NAME ONE THING YOU ARE THANKFUL FOR TODAY AND ASK YOUR PARENT THE SAME QUESTION.

DAY 3

READ PSALM 100

- WHAT DOES THIS PSALM TEACH YOU ABOUT GOD'S CHARACTER?

- IS THERE ANYONE ELSE ON EARTH WHO IS TRULY GOOD LIKE GOD IS?

- DOES THIS PSALM HINT THAT YOU SHOULD BE QUIET ABOUT HIS GOODNESS?

- NAME ONE THING YOU ARE THANKFUL FOR TODAY AND ASK YOUR PARENT THE SAME QUESTION.

DAY 4

READ PSALM 23

WE HAVE READ THREE PSALMS ABOUT SHEEP AND A SHEPHERD. IN WHAT WAY IS GOD YOUR SHEPHERD?

HOW MANY THINGS CAN YOU FIND IN THIS PSALM THAT GOD DOES FOR HIS CHILDREN?

DOES HE ONLY WANT TO DO GOOD TOWARDS YOU?

NAME ONE THING YOU ARE THANKFUL FOR TODAY AND ASK YOUR PARENT THE SAME QUESTION.

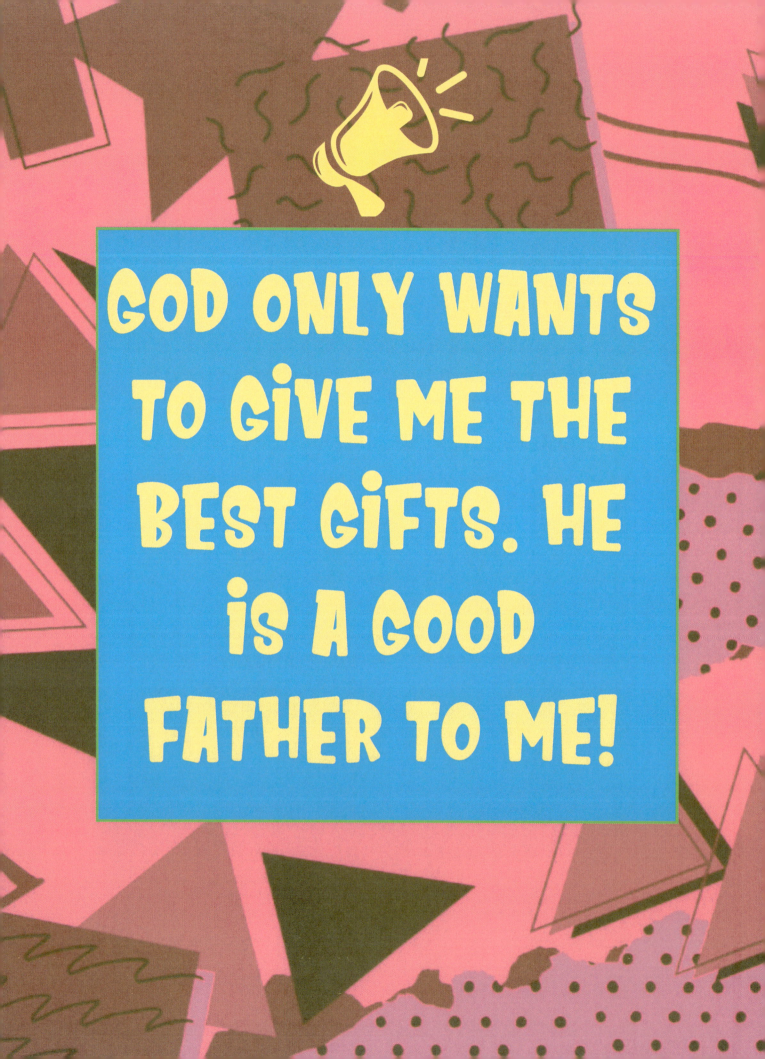

DAY 5

READ JEREMIAH 30:16-24

WHEN THE LORD COMES TO SAVE HIS CHILDREN, WHAT DOES VERSE 19 SAY WILL HAPPEN?

CAN WE BE CLOSE TO GOD OR IS HE SCARY? (VERSE 22)

DOES GOD LOVE TO HEAR YOU LAUGH WITH JOY?

NAME ONE THING YOU ARE THANKFUL FOR TODAY AND ASK YOUR PARENT THE SAME QUESTION.

DAY 6

READ PSALM 34

WHAT SHOULD YOU CONSTANTLY SPEAK?

WHAT DOES GOD DO WHEN WE CALL OUT TO HIM?

CAN YOU REMEMBER A TIME WHEN YOU PRAYED ABOUT SOMETHING AND GOD ANSWERED YOUR PRAYER?

NAME ONE THING YOU ARE THANKFUL FOR TODAY AND ASK YOUR PARENT THE SAME QUESTION.

DAY 7

READ PSALM 46

- IS GOD ALWAYS WILLING TO HELP YOU?

- LOOK UP THE WORDS "REFUGE" AND "STRENGTH." WHAT DOES IT MEAN THAT GOD IS OUR REFUGE AND STRENGTH?

- WHAT ARE SOME THINGS THAT YOU MIGHT BE TEMPTED TO TRUST IN INSTEAD OF TRUSTING IN GOD?

- NAME ONE THING YOU ARE THANKFUL FOR TODAY AND ASK YOUR PARENT THE SAME QUESTION.

DAY 8

READ MATTHEW 6:30-34 AND PHILIPPIANS 4:19

- WHAT DO THESE VERSES TEACH YOU ABOUT YOUR HEAVENLY FATHER?

- DOES HE TEACH YOU TO WORRY?

- WHAT HAS GOD PROVIDED FOR YOU THIS YEAR?

- NAME ONE THING YOU ARE THANKFUL FOR TODAY AND ASK YOUR PARENT THE SAME QUESTION.

DAY 9

READ PSALM 19:7-14

- WHAT WORDS ARE USED IN THIS PSALM TO REFER TO GOD'S WORD?

- WHAT BENEFITS DO YOU EXPERIENCE FROM READING AND OBEYING GOD'S WORD?

- HOW HAS GOD'S WORD HELPED YOU PERSONALLY?

- NAME ONE THING YOU ARE THANKFUL FOR TODAY AND ASK YOUR PARENT THE SAME QUESTION.

DAY 10

READ JAMES 1:17-26

WHAT GOOD THINGS HAS GOD GIVEN YOU?

WHAT DID YOU ENJOY TODAY THAT GOD HAS PROVIDED FOR YOU?

WHAT ARE THE TWO THINGS WE MUST DO WITH GOD'S WORD?

NAME ONE THING YOU ARE THANKFUL FOR TODAY AND ASK YOUR PARENT THE SAME QUESTION.

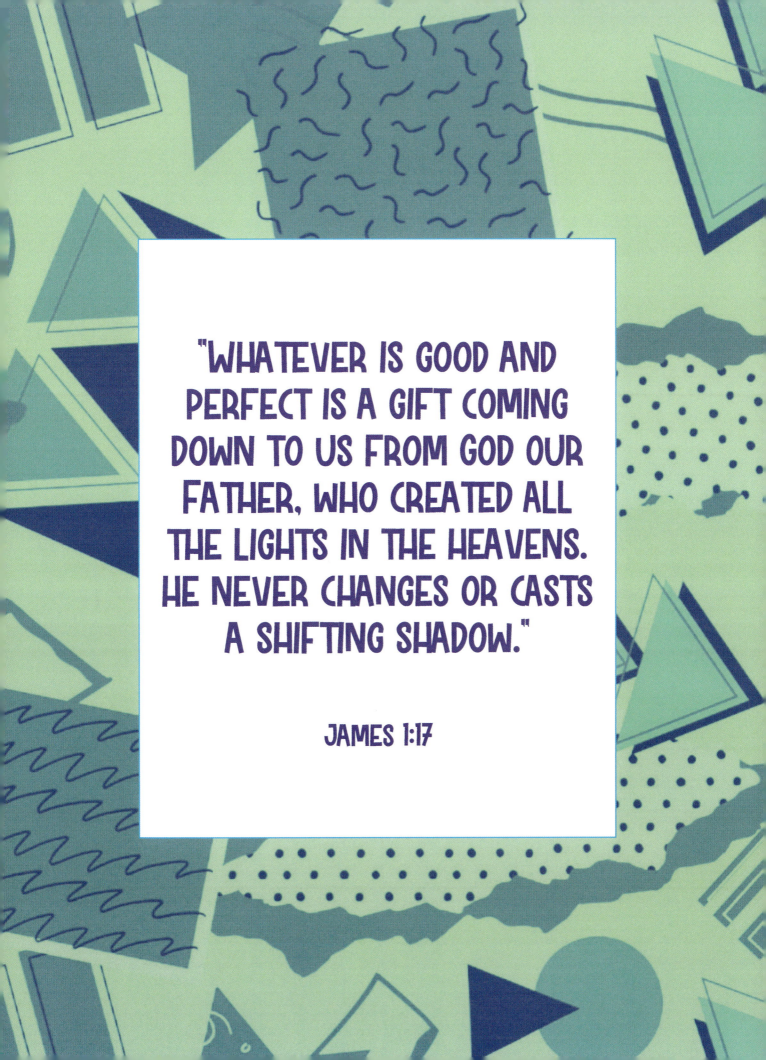

"Whatever is good and perfect is a gift coming down to us from God our Father, who created all the lights in the heavens. He never changes or casts a shifting shadow."

James 1:17

DAY 11

READ LUKE 17:11-19

> HOW MANY LEPERS DID JESUS HEAL? HOW MANY RETURNED TO GIVE THANKS?

> WHAT DID THE LAST LEPER RECEIVE THAT THE OTHER NINE DIDN'T GET?

> IS IT IMPORTANT YOU REMAIN THANKFUL FOR ALL THAT HE HAS DONE FOR YOU?

> NAME ONE THING YOU ARE THANKFUL FOR TODAY AND ASK YOUR PARENT THE SAME QUESTION.

DAY 12

READ PSALM 103:8-22 AND 1 JOHN 1:9

WHAT DOES GOD DO WITH YOUR SIN IF YOU CONFESS IT?

IS IT HARD TO FORGIVE OTHERS?

DOES GOD EVER HOLD BACK FROM FORGIVING YOU?

NAME ONE THING YOU ARE THANKFUL FOR TODAY AND ASK YOUR PARENT THE SAME QUESTION.

DAY 13

READ HEBREWS 11:1-34

WHAT CAN YOU LEARN FROM THE BELIEVERS WHO LIVED DURING BIBLE TIMES?

WHAT WORD DESCRIBES EACH OF THE PEOPLE IN THIS PASSAGE?

IS IT HOW YOU SHOULD LIVE NOW?

NAME ONE THING YOU ARE THANKFUL FOR TODAY AND ASK YOUR PARENT THE SAME QUESTION.

DAY 14

LET'S REVIEW SO FAR!

WHAT HAVE WE LEARNED ABOUT GOD? WHAT ABOUT GOD HAS IMPRESSED YOU THE MOST SO FAR THIS MONTH?

NAME ONE THING YOU ARE THANKFUL FOR TODAY AND ASK YOUR PARENT THE SAME QUESTION.

DAY 15

READ PROVERBS 17:17 AND PROVERBS 27:17

GOOD FRIENDS ARE A GIFT FROM GOD. WHAT FRIENDS ARE YOU THANKFUL FOR?

DO YOU HAVE ANY FRIENDS THAT ENCOURAGE YOU TO BE MORE LIKE CHRIST?

HOW CAN YOU BE A FRIEND THAT HELPS OTHERS TO BE MORE LIKE CHRIST?

NAME ONE THING YOU ARE THANKFUL FOR TODAY AND ASK YOUR PARENT THE SAME QUESTION.

DAY 16

READ 1 THESSALONIANS 5:12-13

WHAT LEADERS ARE IN YOUR LIFE? PASTOR? TEACHERS? WRITE AND SEND A NOTE OF THANKS TO ONE OF YOUR CHURCH LEADERS. PRAY FOR THEM.

NAME ONE THING YOU ARE THANKFUL FOR TODAY AND ASK YOUR PARENT THE SAME QUESTION.

DAY 17

READ 2 CORINTHIANS 5:17 AND PHILIPPIANS 1:3-6

- WHAT DO THESE VERSES TEACH US ABOUT WHAT GOD DOES IN THE LIVES OF BELIEVERS?

- HOW CAN YOU TELL THAT YOU ARE GROWING SPIRITUALLY?

- WHAT ARE SOME THINGS YOU CAN DO TO GET CLOSER TO GOD?

- NAME ONE THING YOU ARE THANKFUL FOR TODAY AND ASK YOUR PARENT THE SAME QUESTION.

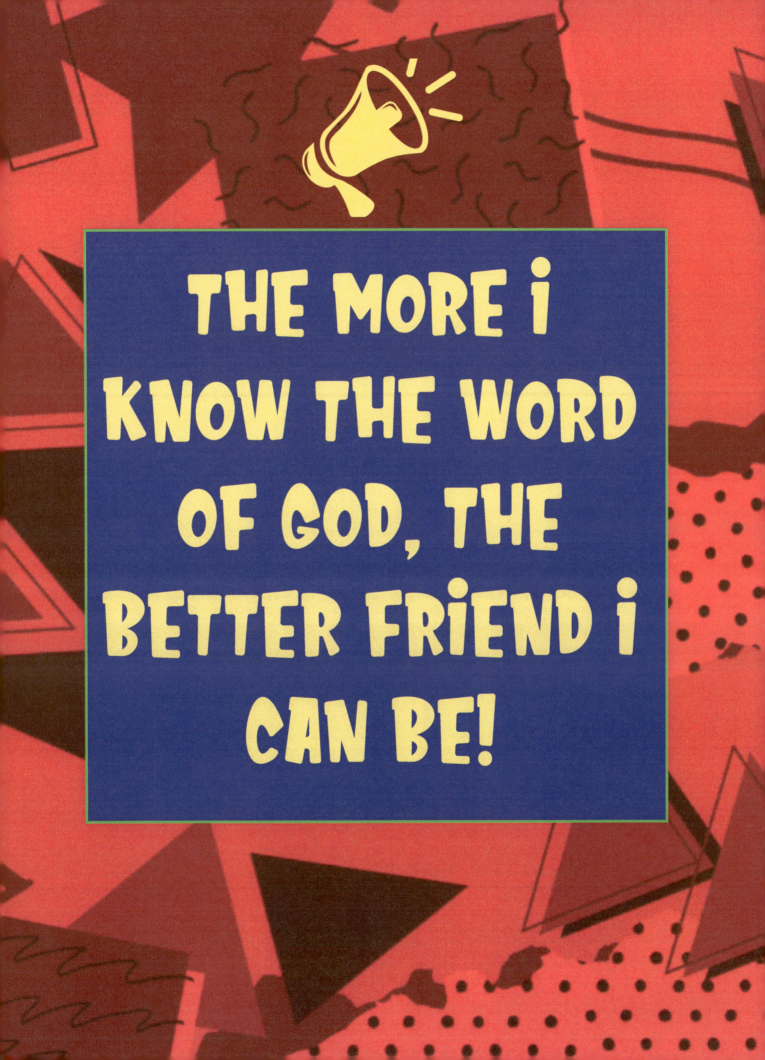

DAY 18

READ PSALM 119:97-106

WHAT BENEFITS OF GOD'S WORD DO WE LEARN ABOUT IN THESE VERSES?

HOW IS GOD'S WORD LIKE A LAMP TO YOUR FEET?

WHAT HAPPENS WHEN WE DON'T OBEY GOD'S WORD?

NAME ONE THING YOU ARE THANKFUL FOR TODAY AND ASK YOUR PARENT THE SAME QUESTION.

DAY 19

READ 1 CHRONICLES 16:7-36

WHY IS DAVID'S SONG OF PRAISE SO IMPORTANT?

IN VERSE 34, WHY SHOULD YOU CONTINUE TO PRAISE THE LORD?

SHOULD WE PRAISE THE LORD EVEN WHEN THINGS MAY NOT FEEL THE GREATEST?

NAME ONE THING YOU ARE THANKFUL FOR TODAY AND ASK YOUR PARENT THE SAME QUESTION.

DAY 20

READ PSALM 8

- YOU CAN APPRECIATE THE BEAUTY IN NATURE BECAUSE YOU ARE CREATED IN GOD'S IMAGE. WHAT ARE SOME THINGS THAT YOU ENJOY DOING IN NATURE?

- WHAT ARE YOU THANKFUL FOR THAT GOD HAS CREATED IN NATURE?

- WHAT IS YOUR FAVORITE SEASON?

- NAME ONE THING YOU ARE THANKFUL FOR TODAY AND ASK YOUR PARENT THE SAME QUESTION.

DAY 21

READ COLOSSIANS 3:15-17

WHAT SHOULD RULE IN YOUR HEART?

WHAT SHOULD YOU CONSTANTLY DO?

HOW DOES THE WORD OF GOD DWELL INSIDE OF US?

NAME ONE THING YOU ARE THANKFUL FOR TODAY AND ASK YOUR PARENT THE SAME QUESTION.

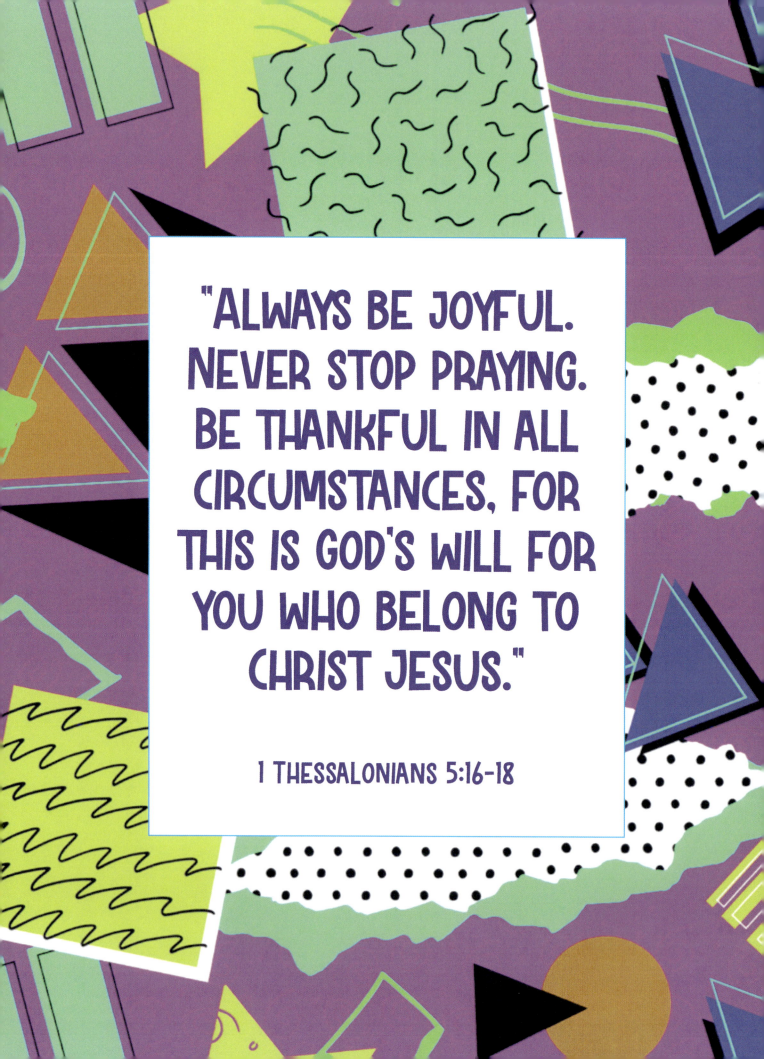

DAY 22

READ 1 THESSALONIANS 5:16-18

WHEN SHOULD WE REJOICE?

WHEN SHOULD WE PRAY?

WHEN SHOULD WE GIVE THANKS?

NAME ONE THING YOU ARE THANKFUL FOR TODAY AND ASK YOUR PARENT THE SAME QUESTION.

DAY 23

READ LAMENTATIONS 3:22-32

WHAT IS NEW EVERY MORNING?

WHAT DOES IT MEAN THAT GOD IS FAITHFUL?

WHAT IS ANOTHER BIBLE VERSE THAT TELLS US GOD IS FAITHFUL?

NAME ONE THING YOU ARE THANKFUL FOR TODAY AND ASK YOUR PARENT THE SAME QUESTION.

DAY 24

READ 1 TIMOTHY 4:4-5 AND 12-14

DID GOD CREATE ANYTHING BAD?

ASK THE LORD TO MAKE YOU A MOUTHPIECE FOR HIM. WHAT CAN YOU SAY TODAY TO EXPLAIN HIS GOODNESS TO OTHERS?

ARE YOU TOO YOUNG TO DO GREAT THINGS FOR GOD?

NAME ONE THING YOU ARE THANKFUL FOR TODAY AND ASK YOUR PARENT THE SAME QUESTION.

DAY 25

READ PHILIPPIANS 4:4-13

WHAT IS VERSE 6 TELLING YOU?

IF YOU REMAIN FAITHFUL AT ALL TIMES WHAT WILL GUARD YOU?

IS THAT A FRUIT OF THE SPIRIT?

NAME ONE THING YOU ARE THANKFUL FOR TODAY AND ASK YOUR PARENT THE SAME QUESTION.

DAY 26
READ PSALM 136

THIS PSALM REHEARSES ALL OF HOW GOD WAS FAITHFUL AND LOVING TO THE NATION OF ISRAEL. MAKE A LIST OF ALL THE WAYS GOD HAS BEEN FAITHFUL TO YOUR FAMILY. THEN PRAY TOGETHER AND THANK HIM FOR WHAT HE HAS DONE!

DAY 27
MAKE A THANKFUL LIST

LIST SOMETHING NEXT TO EACH CATEGORY YOU ARE THANKFUL FOR!

FAMILY

FRIENDS

CHURCH

HOME

MYSELF

NATURE

"But you will receive power when the Holy Spirit comes upon you. And you will be my witnesses, telling people about me everywhere—in Jerusalem, throughout Judea, in Samaria, and to the ends of the earth."

Acts 1:8

THE BOOK OF ACTS

The Book of Acts is unlike anything we have in the New Testament. The book combines a record of the early church's history with speeches, accounts of miraculous events, and action-packed scenes of persecution and triumph. The book's full title is called "The Acts of the Apostles."

This book gives us the history of the early church through the faithful witness of several significant apostles. But Acts isn't just about the acts of these apostles. Ultimately it tells us the story of the Holy Spirit poured out on the apostles on the Day of Pentecost.

We get to see the Holy Spirit, who is the third person of the Trinity, work through humans and the gospel proclaimed despite intense opposition.

Although Jesus was the Son of God from birth, he didn't perform any miracles until he was filled with the Holy Spirit after being baptized by John (Luke 4:1). That's because the power to do supernatural things comes after you're filled with the Holy Spirit (Acts 1:8).

You will learn of the power and presence of the Holy Spirit. He will give you guidance, power, and boldness to carry out all God has for you in this life.

Day 1:

READ: Acts Chapter 1

WRITE: Verse 8

_____

_____

_____

_____

Day 2:

READ: Acts Chapter 2

WRITE: Verses 17-18, 25

_____

_____

_____

_____

_____

_____

Day 3:

READ: Acts Chapter 3

WRITE: Verse 16

_____

_____

Day 4:

READ: Acts Chapter 4

WRITE: Verse 12

_____

_____

Day 5:

READ: Acts Chapter 5

WRITE: Verse 16

_____

_____

Day 6:

READ: Acts Chapter 6

WRITE: Verse 8

_____

_____

_____

Day 7:

READ: Acts Chapter 7

WRITE: Verse 46

_____

_____

_____

Something to think about: How do you find favor with God?

_____

_____

_____

_____

Acts 6:8

"_____, a _____
(Your name)   (boy or girl)

full of God's grace and power, performed amazing miracles and signs among the people."

Day 8:

READ: Acts Chapter 8

WRITE: Verse 17

_____

_____

What is one way you can receive the Holy Spirit?

_____

_____

Day 9:

READ: Acts Chapter 9

WRITE: Verse 22

_____

_____

What made Saul's preaching grow in power? (Hint verse 17.)

_____

_____

Day 10:

READ: Acts Chapter 10

WRITE: Verse 38

_____

_____

_____

Does Jesus heal all people or only certain people?

_____

Day 11:

READ: Acts Chapter 11

WRITE: Verse 23-24

_____

_____

_____

Day 12:

READ: Acts Chapter 12

WRITE: Verse 11

_____

_____

_____

Day 13:

READ: Acts Chapter 13

WRITE: Verse 47

_____

_____

_____

Day 14:

READ: Acts Chapter 14

WRITE: Verse 3

_____

_____

_____

What did the Lord prove in that verse?

_____

_____

_____

Day 15:

READ: Acts Chapter 15

WRITE: Verses 8-9

_____

_____

_____

_____

_____

Day 16:

READ: Acts Chapter 16

WRITE: Verse 18

_____

_____

_____

Understand why Paul did what he did in this verse. Paul got exasperated (intensely irritated and frustrated) with the situation around him so he commanded the evil spirit to leave. We have the same power when we are filled with the Holy Spirit.

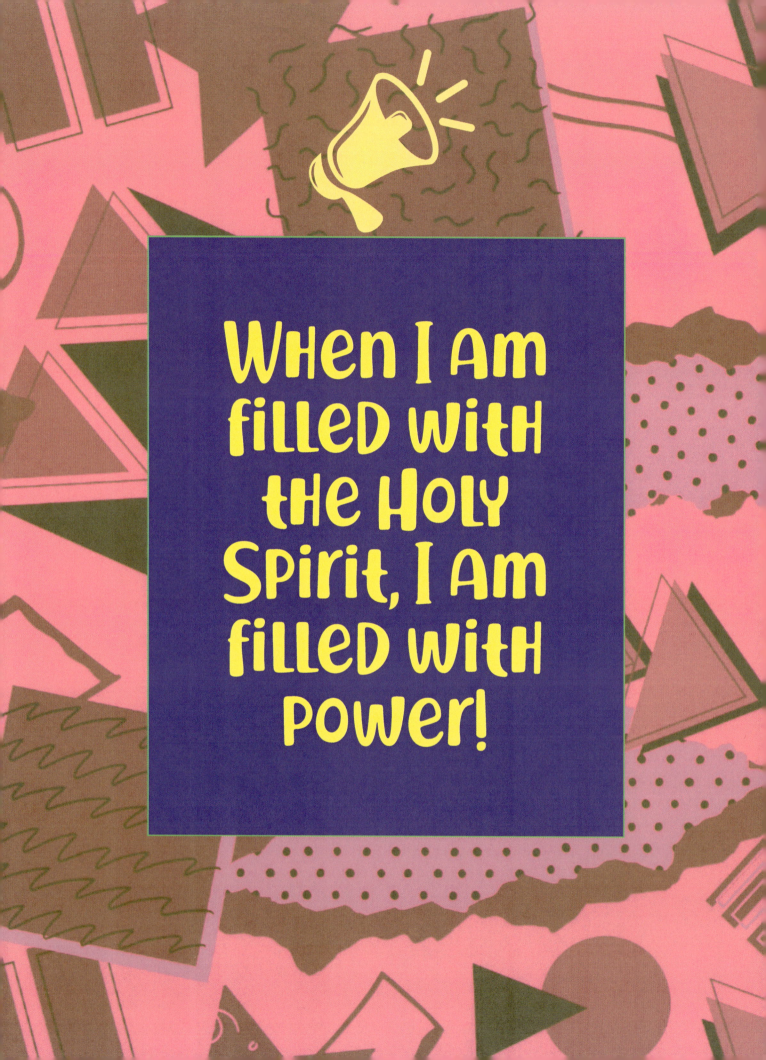

Day 17:

READ: Acts Chapter 17

WRITE: Verses 30-31

_____

_____

_____

Day 18:

READ: Acts Chapter 18

WRITE: Verses 9-10

_____

_____

_____

Day 19:

READ: Acts Chapter 19

WRITE: Verses 5-6

_____

_____

_____

Something to think about:

Take a look at Acts 19:13-16.

It shows how our identity looks in the spirit realm. Look at the difference between the Seven Sons of Sceva, Paul, and Jesus.

The Holy Spirit that filled Paul and Jesus was evident to the evil spirit. The man with the evil spirit realized he shouldn't mess with Paul and Jesus. The seven men who had no authority in the spirit were attacked, beaten and even stripped naked.

Day 20:
READ: Acts Chapter 20
WRITE: Verse 32

_____

_____

Day 21:
READ: Acts Chapter 21
WRITE: Verse 13

_____

_____

Day 22:

READ: Acts Chapter 22

WRITE: Verse 16

_____
_____
_____
_____

Day 23:

READ: Acts Chapter 23

WRITE: Verse 11

_____
_____
_____
_____

As you read the verse replace the names Jerusalem and Rome with your hometown and another place where you should win souls. Make a point to tell others around you about Jesus! The Holy Spirit gives you boldness to do so.

Day 24:

READ: Acts Chapter 24

WRITE: Verses 14-16

Day 25:

READ: Acts Chapter 25

WRITE: Verse 27

Day 26:

READ: Acts Chapter 26

WRITE: Verses 16-18

Day 27:

READ: Acts Chapter 27

WRITE: Verse 22

_____

_____

_____

Day 28:

READ: Acts Chapter 28

WRITE: Verse 5

_____

_____

_____

We have to look at it like this. When the enemy tries to attack us we have to go shake him off. We have the power to overcome the enemy!

You read the entire book of Acts this month! Way to go!

Day 29:

What was your favorite verse in Acts?

_____

_____

"This means that anyone who belongs to Christ has become a new person. The old life is gone; a new life has begun."

2 Corinthians 5:17

MY IDENTITY IN JESUS

Have you ever had a fingerprint taken? There are many natural things that the world uses to prove our identity—who we really are. But did you know that you have an identity in Jesus?

2 Corinthians 5:17 says, "This means that anyone who belongs to Christ has become a new person. The old life is gone; a new life has begun!"

When you become a Christian, it means that you have a new identity in him! Not just any old boring identity either. You now have a really amazing one!

Do you know how you find out what cool things are included in your new identity? You learn about your new identity in the Word of God! Who does the Bible say that you are? Do you know?

This month, we are going to learn who God says you are and what he says you can have. You are strong, brave, smart, wise, beautiful, handsome, healthy, and so much more!

Day 1:

SAY THIS: I am strong.

READ & WRITE: Deuteronomy 31:6

_____

_____

Day 2:

SAY THIS: I am smart.

READ & WRITE: Proverbs 2:6-7

_____

_____

_____

Day 3:

SAY THIS: I am set apart.

READ & WRITE: 1 Peter 2:9

_____

_____

_____

Day 1:

Day 4:
SAY THIS: I am victorious.
READ & WRITE: Psalm 18:35

Day 5:
SAY THIS: I am free.
READ & WRITE: Galatians 5:1

Day 6:
SAY THIS: I am God's child.
READ & WRITE: 1 John 3:1

Day 7:

SAY THIS: I am forgiven.

READ & WRITE: 1 Peter 2:24

_____

_____

_____

Day 8:

SAY THIS: I am a house for the Holy Spirit.

READ & WRITE: 1 Corinthians 6:19-20

_____

_____

_____

Day 9:

SAY THIS: I am confident in my future.

READ & WRITE: Matthew 6:25-34

_____

_____

_____

Day 10:

SAY THIS: I walk in divine health.

READ & WRITE: Acts 10:38

_____

_____

_____

Day 11:

SAY THIS: I am God's masterpiece.

READ & WRITE: Ephesians 2:10

_____

_____

_____

Day 12:

SAY THIS: I am brand new.

READ & WRITE: 2 Corinthians 5:17

_____

_____

_____

Day 13:

SAY THIS: I am never alone.

READ & WRITE: Isaiah 41:10

_____

_____

Day 14:

SAY THIS: God will always take care of me.

READ & WRITE: Philippians 4:19

_____

_____

_____

Day 15:

SAY THIS: God cares about the things I like.

READ & WRITE: Psalm 37:4

_____

_____

_____

Day 16:

SAY THIS: I produce fruit for the kingdom of God.

READ & WRITE: John 15:7-8

_____

_____

_____

Day 17:

SAY THIS: I have peace in my mind.

READ & WRITE: John 14:27

_____

_____

_____

Day 18:

SAY THIS: My thoughts are about Jesus and his goodness.

READ & WRITE: Isaiah 26:3

_____

_____

_____

Day 19:

SAY THIS: God directs my steps. He will always tell me where to go.

READ & WRITE: Psalm 37:23-24

_____

_____

Day 20:

SAY THIS: I will never have a weak spirit.

READ & WRITE: Isaiah 40:31

_____

_____

Day 21:

SAY THIS: I carry blessings, not burdens.

READ & WRITE: Matthew 11:28-29

_____

_____

Day 22:

SAY THIS: I do not worry about anything.

READ & WRITE: Philippians 4:6

_____

_____

_____

Day 23:

SAY THIS: I stay calm.

READ & WRITE: Exodus 14:14

_____

_____

_____

Day 24:

SAY THIS: I always honor my parents.

READ & WRITE: Exodus 20:12

_____

_____

_____

Day 25:

SAY THIS: God gives me wisdom when I ask.

READ & WRITE: James 1:5

_____

_____

Day 26:

SAY THIS: I will show God's love to every person I meet.

READ & WRITE: John 3:16

_____

_____

_____

Day 27:

SAY THIS: I will always obey the Word of God.

READ & WRITE: Deuteronomy 28:1

_____

_____

_____

Day 28:

SAY THIS: God is always willing to answer my prayers.

READ & WRITE: Mark 11:24

_____

_____

_____

Day 29:

SAY THIS: I am brave and courageous.

READ & WRITE: Joshua 1:9

_____

_____

_____

Day 30:

SAY THIS: God keeps no good thing from me.

READ & WRITE: Psalm 84:11

_____

_____

_____

"There the child grew up healthy and **strong**. He was filled with **wisdom**, and God's **favor** was on him."

Luke 2:40

THE BOOK OF LUKE

The first four books of the New Testament are called the Gospels. They each tell the story of Jesus from a different person's perspective. This month, we are going to do an in-depth study on the book of Luke!

We will do a lot of reading this month, and we have questions for you to answer that will help you really understand what was happening. You will read through the birth of Jesus through to his resurrection!

There are endless things we can learn just from the life of Jesus in these chapters. You are going to read how Jesus was a healer and did miracles! You are going to learn how Jesus reacted to the devil's temptations and how he always stood firm.

You will learn about how he gave his life for you on the cross and died for your sins so you could live in freedom! And you will read how Jesus didn't stay in the tomb but was resurrected and now sits at the right hand of God in Heaven. As we finish this 12-month study, we are going to take a look at Jesus' life and learn how to be more like him!

Day 1: Read Luke Chapter 1

What was Zechariah and Elizabeth's son's name?

_____

What did the angel tell them about their son?

_____

What is the name of the angel that visited Mary?

_____

What did the angel tell Mary?

_____

Day 2: Read Luke Chapter 2

What is the name of the town where Jesus was born?

_____

Who gave Jesus his name?

_____

Who came to visit Jesus after he was born?

_____

Write out Luke 2:40: This is our theme verse for Miracle Word Kids! You are strong, smart, and set apart!

_____

_____

Day 3: Read Luke Chapter 3

How old was Jesus when he began his ministry?

_____

What did John the Baptist mean in verse 16?

_____

_____

Day 4: Read Luke Chapter 4

How many days was Jesus tempted by the devil in the wilderness?

_____

What thing did the devil ask Jesus to turn to bread?

_____

Did Jesus ever give in to the devil's temptations?

_____

What was Peter's mother-in-law's sickness?

_____

Did Jesus heal her?

_____

Day 5 : Read Luke Chapter 5

What did Jesus preach from in verse 3?

_____

At first, there was no fish, but when Jesus gave an instruction to cast the nets, what happened?

_____

_____

What two other types of people does Jesus heal before Chapter 5 ends?

_____

Day 6: Read Luke Chapter 6

Explain verses 46-49:

_____

_____

_____

_____

_____

Day 7: Read Luke Chapter 7

What was wrong with the widow's son in verses 11-17?

_____

What saved the woman in verse 50?

_____

Day 8: Read Luke Chapter 8

There are four types of ground listed in verses 4-8. The ground represents us as a person. Out of the four types, what ground do we need to be?

_____

In verse 48 what do we need to have to receive healing?

_____

Day 9: Read Luke Chapter 9

Jesus preached in front of a large crowd. They all got hungry. How many did he feed that day?

_____

What did he use to feed them all?

_____

How many baskets were filled with the excess food Jesus multiplied?

_____

Day 10: Read Luke Chapter 10

Has Jesus given us ALL power over the devil? (Hint: verse 19.)

_____

In verses 25-37 which of the three men are we to be most like? The priest, the Levite, or the Samaritan? Why?

_____

_____

Day 11: Read Luke Chapter 11

Memorize the Lord's prayer. Say it daily!

The Lord's Prayer

Jesus said, "This is how you should pray:
Father, may your name be kept holy.
May your kingdom come soon.
Give us each day the food we need,
And forgive us our sins,
As we forgive those who sin against us.
And don't let us yield to temptation.

In verse 28 how did Jesus say we can stay blessed?

_____

_____

Day 12: Read Luke Chapter 12

What do Verses 22-31 tell us about being anxious? Why do we never have to fear about being without?

___

___

___

Day 13: Read Luke Chapter 13

How many years did the woman have a disabling spirit?

___

Did Jesus heal her?

___

Did it take him a long time to heal her?

___

What did she do after she was healed?

___

___

Day 14: Read Luke Chapter 14

In the parable of the wedding feast, Jesus is teaching us about humility. We will sit at a place of

_____ if we humble ourselves.

In the parable of the banquet, what is Jesus instructing us to do?

_____

Will people make excuses about not wanting Jesus in their life?

_____

Does that mean we should stop asking them?

_____

Day 15: Read Luke Chapter 15

In the parable of the lost sheep, who do the sheep represent?

_____

Who does the shepherd represent?

_____

Are we to rejoice differently if 100 people get saved versus one person?

_____

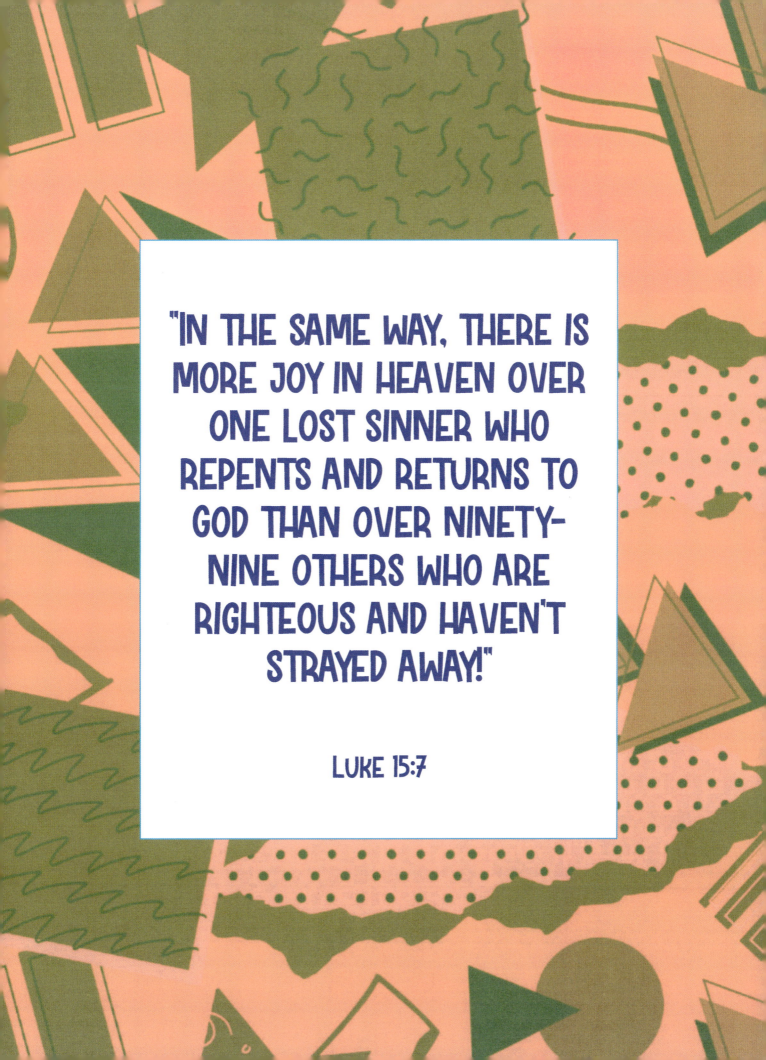

"In the same way, there is more joy in heaven over one lost sinner who repents and returns to God than over ninety-nine others who are righteous and haven't strayed away!"

Luke 15:7

Day 16: Read Luke Chapter 16

Should we care more about what people think about us or what Jesus thinks?

_____

Does God know our hearts?

_____

Day 17: Read Luke Chapter 17

Will we be tempted by sin?

_____

Do we have to follow through with the temptation?

_____

What does the Bible say the size of our faith can be and still see results?

_____

How many lepers did Jesus cleanse?

_____

Because one of the men stayed in praise and thanksgiving and returned to Jesus, what happened to him?

_____

Day 18: Read Luke Chapter 18

Does Jesus love children?

___

Did the disciples assume the children were bothering Jesus?

___

What did Jesus do about it?

___

The rich young ruler was sad. Was he sad because he had money, or because Jesus told him to sell it all and follow him?

___

Does what Jesus said to the rich young ruler mean you can't be rich as a Christian?

___

Jesus wants to show us in this story that the rich young ruler's _____ were more important than Jesus.

Day 19: Read Luke Chapter 19

Who was Zacchaeus?

___

What type of tree did Zacchaeus climb?

___

Why did the people in the crowd complain that Jesus wanted to stay with Zacchaeus?

___

What good thing came out of Jesus going to Zacchaeus's house?

___

Why did Jesus get mad in the Temple?

___

Did Jesus stop them or leave them alone?

___

Day 20: Read Luke Chapter 20

Who did the people pay their taxes to?

___

Trick question- what did they call the money during that time?

___

Were the scribes and chief priests trying to trick Jesus?

___

Day 21: Read Luke Chapter 21

In verses 34-36 how is Jesus telling us to behave?

___

Should we wait until we are adults to pray?

___

Day 22: Read Luke Chapter 22

Who was the disciple that betrayed Jesus?

_____

What did Judas agree to receive to turn Jesus in?

_____

What was the Passover?

_____

What did they do during the Lord's Supper?

_____

What do the bread and juice represent?

_____

Where did Jesus go to pray?

_____

Did Jesus ask to not die?

_____

Who strengthened him to move forward?

_____

Does one of his disciples deny him? _____

Who? _____

Day 23: Read Luke Chapter 23

Did Pilate and Herod want to punish Jesus at first?

_____

Did Pilate and Herod find Jesus guilty of a crime?

_____

What changed their minds to crucify Jesus?

_____

Did they hurt Jesus on the way to the hill? _____

With what? _____

What was the name of the place where they hung Jesus on the cross?

_____

Did they kill Jesus or did he give up his own spirit? (Hint: verse 46.)

_____

Where did they lay his body after he died?

_____

Day 24: Read Luke Chapter 24

Who went to the tomb early Sunday morning?

What did they find?

Was someone else at the tomb?

Did Jesus appear to his disciples again?

What did Jesus do to the disciples right before being carried up to Heaven?

CONGRATULATIONS

You did it! You have completed a whole year of Bible Study with Miracle Word Kids! We are so proud of you. Never lose your hunger to know more of the truth. Knowing and obeying the Word of God will keep you strong, smart, and set apart! When you do what God says, you will be successful in everything.

ACKNOWLEDGMENTS

To Dad and Mom,
Thank you for raising me to love the Lord with my whole heart. It now continues to the next generation.

"And this is my covenant with them," says the Lord. "My Spirit will not leave them, and neither will these words I have given you. They will be on your lips and on the lips of your children and your children's children forever. I, the Lord, have spoken! -Isaiah 59:21

To Ted,
You push me out of my comfort zone. Thank you for helping me do things I never saw myself stepping into. I'm grateful for you and I love you eternally.

To Tiffany,
Thank you for the countless hours of hard work you spent to get this devotional into the hands of the younger generation so they'll know God's word. Love you, friend!

Made in the USA
Middletown, DE
11 October 2023

40260591R00124